Creative Approaches to Social Work Practice Learning

Other books you may be interested in:

Innovations in Practice Learning
Edited by Sue Taplin 978-1-912096-12-1

Dilemmas and Decision Making in Social Work
Abbi Jackson 978-1-914171-20-8

Social Work and Covid-19: Lessons for Education and Practice
Edited by Denise Turner 978-1-913453-61-9

Out of the Shadows: The Role of Social Workers in Disasters
Edited by Angie Bartoli, Maris Stratulis and
Rebekah Pierre 978-1-915080-07-3

The Anti-racist Social Worker: Stories of Activism by Social Care and Allied Health Professionals
Edited by Tanya Moore and Glory Simango 978-1-914171-41-3

CRITICAL PUBLISHING

Creative Approaches to Social Work Practice Learning

Edited by

Heidi Dix and Aisha Howells

First published in 2022 by Critical Publishing Ltd

British Library Cataloguing in Publication Data
A CIP record for this book is available from the British Library

ISBN: 978-1-915080-01-1

This book is also available in the following e-book formats:
EPUB ISBN: 978-1-915080-02-8
Adobe e-book ISBN: 978-1-915080-03-5

Cover and text design by Out of House and Lauren Carr
Project management by Newgen Publishing UK
Printed and bound in Great Britain by 4edge, Essex

Critical Publishing
3 Connaught Road
St Albans
AL3 5RX

www.criticalpublishing.com

Printed on FSC accredited paper

Contents

Acknowledgements

We would like to recognise the members of the social work practice learning planning conference committee, who were the inspiration for the creation of this book and who manage to generate an amazing annual festival for practice educators each year.

We would also like to thank Lauren Carr for creating such beautiful illustrations which really help to bring each tool to life.

We would also like to show gratitude to the poets whose work appears throughout this book for generously sharing their poetry with us and of course we need to acknowledge the wonderfully creative chapter authors. A mention also needs to be made to the early reviewers and whose constructive, wise feedback helped to shape the direction of the book - you know who you are.

This book is dedicated to social work practice educators, on-site supervisors and students whose contribution to social work education is often underestimated. We see you and celebrate you!

Meet the editors

Heidi Dix is a senior lecturer in social work at the University of Suffolk, as well as the lead for quality assurance and practice development in a local authority Youth Justice Service. She is also the safeguarding trustee for Outreach Youth, a charitable incorporated organisation for children and young people who identify as LGBTQIA+. Her interests include social work practice learning and relational, trauma-informed practice.

Aisha Howells is a senior lecturer in social work at the University of Suffolk. She is a registered social worker interested in understanding the world through a critical lens and passionate about carrying out research in child and family social work, trauma and abuse, lived experience, narrative approaches and practice education. An experienced practice educator, Aisha's love for creativity in learning underpins her entire teaching approach.

Meet the contributors

Illustrations

Lauren Carr leads an Art, Design and Technology faculty in a secondary school in Suffolk. Lauren has written articles for NSEAD's AD magazine and for the International Journal of Art Education. She has been involved in the National Society for Art Education's drawing initiative 'Thinking, Expression, Action' and through this, became part of a national sketch-book circle. Lauren continues to complete commissioned drawings and other drawing projects.

Chapters

Claire Skilleter is a Practice Education Lead in the Suffolk and Norfolk Teaching Partnership in the UK. Claire has over 30 years' experience working with children and families and is a qualified social worker and practice educator. In her current role Claire supports students, practice educators, and on-site supervisors in Norfolk County Council. Claire is particularly interested in relationship based social work and creative methods for working with students, individuals, and families. Claire regularly presents her work at practice education training events both locally in Norfolk and Suffolk and nationally. In 2021, Claire was named Practice Educator of the Year in the Social Worker of the Year Awards.

Anna Wright is a lecturer in social work at the University of East Anglia. Anna qualified as a social worker in 2010 and has been a practice educator since 2015. She has worked in local authorities as a social worker, manager and, most recently, in a service improvement team with particular focus on developing best practice for the support of newly qualified social workers, students, practice educators and on-site supervisors. Her interests are in creative approaches to social work education and in developing reflective supervisory practice. Outside of work Anna enjoys swimming outdoors and pottering on her allotment.

Garfield Hunt started his career in social care in 1990, working in residential care with adolescents. During his career, he has worked across the statutory, voluntary and private sectors, and before entering academia, worked as an independent social worker. His teaching interests include anti-discrimination, anti-oppression, anti-racism, equality and diversity, leaving care, housing and homelessness, developmental psychology and safeguarding/child protection. He has particular interests in outcomes for fostered and adopted children, for care leavers and student feedback and engagement. Garfield is passionate about the experiences of 'global majorities' staff and students in education (primary school to level 7).

Alison Taylor is mother to a 24-year-old man who was diagnosed with an autism spectrum disorder at the age of two. She is also completing a PhD in resilience with mothers of children with autism as a case study and working as an academic. Alison believes that people learn by being able to relate stories to their own lives and seeing how that helps to apply the theories. By sharing her own story and ideas, Alison hopes to build bridges between people with lived experience and those who provide services.

Nora Duckett is a registered social worker and academic with 18 years practice-based knowledge and experience, predominately in services for children and families. Since 2004 Nora has worked as an educator in higher education. Nora's research interests reflect her practice-based experiences and focus on improving understandings of professional dangerousness in child protection social work education and practice.

Caroline Aldridge is currently a freelance speaker and trainer, and an experienced children and families social worker, practice educator and lecturer. Her qualifications include: BA (Hons) Social Work, MA in Advanced Social Work, Diploma in Teaching and Education, and Fellow of the Higher Education Academy. She is part-way through a professional doctorate in Health and Social Care. Caroline is author of *He Died Waiting: Learning the Lessons – A Bereaved Mother's View of Mental Health Services.* More information about Caroline is on her website www.learningsocialworker.com and she can be contacted via Twitter @CarolineAldrid5

Poems

Angela Bell is a second-year undergraduate mature student, studying a BA (Hons) in English Literature and Linguistics at the University of Suffolk. She has a love for the written and spoken word and hopes to move into a career based in the field of linguistics, with particular interest in speech and language therapy of aphasia patients. She has enjoyed reading classic British literature during her studies and has developed a new-found appreciation for dystopian novels as well as modernist texts of the early twentieth century.

Demi Bowler is a proud mum of two wonderful children and has been writing poetry since her teenage years. Whenever troubled in life, she has turned to verse and poetry to help as an important part of healing and recovery. Demi's 20-year career as a singer and performer has strengthened her passion for lyrics, being able to connect with people encompassing a multitude of emotions. Demi describes poetry as her therapy to release thoughts with pen and paper and feels privileged to share her words with you.

Makayla Bowler is an 18-year-old singer/songwriter who has achieved four A levels (two of which are in languages) and has begun to teach English to students all over the world as a second language. She has always had a passion for languages and expressing the way she feels through writing and, ultimately, storytelling. With personal experience and a unique perspective being the driving force behind Makayla's work, she feels honoured to share with you a few of the many words which she has written but never got the chance to say.

Alison Dudeney joined the Adventures in Creative Writing course at Cardiff University in 1999 with the legendary British Beat-poet Chris Torrance. It was a revelation; experimenting with word and thought set her firmly on the path to becoming a writer. In 2020, after leaving a career in management, she began her MA in Creative and Critical Writing at the University of Suffolk. She writes short stories and poetry and is currently working on a novel set in the Second World War.

Amanda Hodgkinson is an award-winning novelist, poet and a Senior Lecturer in Creative Writing at the University of Suffolk. Her writing has been published in 17 languages and is focused on place, memory, family and the dynamics of love.

Lanai Collis-Phillips is 20 years old and studying at university to become a children's nurse. She believes that everyone can play a role in fighting systemic and institutional injustice and believes this is easier to do when we work together.

Introduction

Heidi Dix and Aisha Howells

People work in different ways and learn in different ways.
(Student 8B, Howells and Bald, 2020)

Creativity in social work is discussed in many different spaces and in a variety of ways. As social work is a profession underpinned by human rights and social justice, social workers are often required to find creative ways to work collaboratively with children, adults and communities to support them to access and enact their rights and entitlements. There is also a long-standing debate as to whether social work is an *art* or a *science*, with evidence-informed approaches often depicted at one end of the spectrum and innovation and creativity deemed to be at the other. These ideas are sometimes discussed among concerns that the profession has become managerial and overly bureaucratic, leaving social workers frustrated that too much of their time is taken up doing administrative tasks and leaving little capacity to work relationally with others in line with the values of the profession. Conversely, the request that social workers themselves need to be more creative is often espoused by various government departments and organisations in response to their lack of investment and chronic under-resourcing of human services.

Creativity involves an ability to create new ideas and problem solve in a novel way. Requiring both originality and value, it is about both offering a fresh perspective and being useful in some way. It is suggested that creativity is something that cannot be taught but exists within all of us and requires inspiration and opportunities to flourish. An example of this can be found in early 2020, where due to the challenges brought about by the Covid-19 pandemic, practice educators, on-site supervisors and students found innovative ways to engage with learning and teaching in a digital world. Yet, perhaps many of these people would not have described themselves as creative individuals prior to this experience. The same can be said for some of the contributors to this book who would not consider themselves to be particularly creative, but due to their passion for a particular area of interest have produced original resources for you to use in social work practice learning.

A brief overview of the book contents

The intention of this book is to provide a resource for practice educators and students to support learning and teaching. Each chapter contains standalone tools that can be used in the practice learning placement. As well as providing a brief description of each tool, with examples of how it can be used within practice learning and on many occasions in social work practice more widely, the author(s) of each chapter describe the inspiration behind their innovation. Each chapter also provides a brief outline of the theoretical ideas and/or concepts that underpin the tools they have developed. Aspects of each chapter have been illustrated to enable easy identification of the different features so that you can dip in and out of the book as needed. In the appendices, a copy of the tool has been provided for you and the student to easily access.

Interwoven between many of the chapters are original pieces of poetry or spoken word. We suggest that these poems can be used to support learning, teaching and assessment in a way that works for both practice educators and students.

The book attempts to mirror the journey of the practice learning opportunity and so **Chapter 1** sees Claire Skilleter discussing the importance of beginning well through establishing an effective relationship. Using the different components of a chair, Skilleter discusses how a safe environment can be created to enable students to undertake their best learning. Skilleter also provides an innovative way to capture and record the achievements of the student as the practice learning opportunity progresses.

Awareness of digital poverty and the impact of this is increasing, and in **Chapter 2**, Anna Wright provides simple yet fun activities to help practice educators and on-site supervisors explore this subject with students as well as any accessibility issues they may be experiencing. Wright also highlights the importance of a 'team around the student' approach and provides a helpful checklist that can be used to prepare the team for the student joining them.

Anti-racist practice has a long-established history in social work. The murder of George Floyd in 2020 reinvigorated the profession's commitment to anti-racism and in **Chapter 3** Garfield Hunt outlines tools to help all involved in practice learning to consider their understanding and experience of racism, as well as highlighting the need to always promote and actively engage in anti-racist social work practice.

In **Chapter 4,** Caroline Aldridge highlights the importance of providing a trauma-informed environment to enable students to understand and make sense of their own experiences as part of an exploration of self. Aldridge takes established tools used within social work, such as chronologies and timelines, and translates these to the practice learning setting to provide innovative ways they can be used to support learning and teaching.

Being a practice educator in social work can be a lonely endeavour with social work practitioners having to undertake the task on top of their usual roles and responsibilities, with little support from the organisation and limited professional development opportunities available to them (Plenty and Gower, 2013). As such, **Chapter 5**, by Heidi Dix and Aisha Howells, provides a tool which outlines a set of reflective activities to enable practice educators to consider their motivation and commitment to students, as well as helping them to explore how comfortable they feel with the legitimate authority they hold within the role. This chapter also provides a tool to help students and practice educators create a rights-based culture within their social work practice.

Narrative approaches and storytelling are used within social work practice, and in **Chapter 6,** Alison Taylor recounts her experiences in the form of vignettes as a way to encourage practice educators and students to build confidence and consider their well-being to develop into autonomous professionals.

In **Chapter 7**, Nora Duckett discusses the importance of professional curiosity in social work and provides reflective activities in the form of checklists that can be used by practice educators and students to explore assumptions, understand aspects of professional dangerousness and help the development of professional curiosity.

Finally, **Chapter 8** sees Claire Skilleter discussing the importance of endings in social work and provides several innovative ways to support students to end their work with people with lived experience effectively. The chapter also provides a tool to support both practice educators and students to mark the end of the practice learning opportunity.

Going forward, we suspect that some aspects of practice learning will continue to occur virtually for the foreseeable future. Like some of the contributors to this book, you may not initially consider yourself to be a 'creative' person. However, we hope to take you on a journey of discovery and through engaging with the tools outlined in the chapters, you will become inspired to explore this side of yourself. We actively encourage you to utilise both your unconscious and conscious mind to release your inner creativity and, in turn, motivate students to release theirs and participate in imaginative social work practice learning.

References

Howells, A and Bald, C (2020) 'This Is My Oasis': An Exploration of Student Hub Support for Social Work Students' Wellbeing. *Social Work Education*. https://doi.org/10.1080/02615479.2020.1861242

Plenty, J and Gower, D (2013) The Reform of Social Work Practice Education and Training and Supporting Practice Educators. *The Journal of Practice Teaching and Learning*, 12(2): 48–66.

A note about illustrations

This book is centred on different and diverse creative approaches. Both of us, as editors, are visual learners where our learning is often enriched with visual elements. As such, we have repeated illustrations throughout the chapters indicating specific sections that we believe are important for you as practice educators and students to know, so that you can use the tools to their maximum potential. Although the names of the headings may be different or appear in a different order within each chapter, the illustrations reflect the details in the boxes below.

	**Tool** An introduction to the tool. This provides a brief *overview*.
	**Inspiration** Where the inspiration for the tool is drawn from. This is the tool's *origins*.
	**Theory** The theoretical perspective which underpins the tool. This is social work practice being *evidence informed*.
	**Example** Where an example is provided of the tool being used. This brings the *tool to life*.
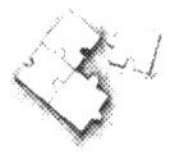	**Application** The description of putting the tool into practice in learning and teaching. This is the *how-to*.
	**Social work practice** Shows you how to use the tool in your work with people with lived experience. This is about your *day-to-day practice*.
	**Three key points** Outlines three key take-away learning points. This is the *summary*.
	**Poem** This is a further *learning tool* to use within the practice educator and student relationship.

Chapter 1

Let's start at the beginning

Claire Skilleter

In the beginning...

This chapter will look at the importance of beginning student practice learning opportunities and working relationships well, thus setting the scene for ending well. In fact, Kadushin (1990) suggests that the beginning is where preparations for endings should start. The start of the practice learning opportunity and the relationship between the practice educator and the student is, in part, the beginning of the end. It is here, at the start, where we already know when our supervisory relationship will end. As such, the beginning of the practice learning opportunity is best placed to create a relationship of safety and trust, which are the underpinnings to end well. Put simply, getting these basics right, from the start, shapes the supervisory relationship and the path it may follow.

In terms of practice educators and students working together from the outset, McMullin's (2017) model for relationship building is transferrable to the student practice learning process. The model has four stages, all of which need attention and are of equal importance:

- engage;
- negotiate;
- enable;
- ending.

The model is not meant to be prescriptive and all relationships are unique. However, the model is helpful in breaking down the process of relationship building (McColgan and McMullin, 2017). To apply the model to the practice educator and student relationship, the practice educator and student begin the practice learning opportunity by *engaging* with each other maybe through a pre-placement meeting, a supervision agreement and getting to know each other activities. As part of the practice learning agreement and throughout the placement the practice educator and student *negotiate* the learning opportunities. The practice educator then *enables* the student to develop learning through practice and the use of supervision. Finally, there is an *'ending'*; the practice educator writes the final report and makes their final assessment. Work with people with lived experience draws to a close and the working relationship between the practice educator and the students ends. Sometimes when things go wrong, there are enforced endings which happen earlier than planned. For example, the student withdraws or does not pass the practice learning opportunity and it is terminated. When this happens, the ending is likely to be painful for both student and practice educator and the opportunity to 'de-brief' and reflect on the experience is likely to be vital for both the student and practice educator.

This chapter will pay attention to the 'engage' stage of relationship building, but also has an eye on the ending stage (which is further discussed in Chapter 8). McColgan and McMullin (2017) state that potential endings should be discussed at the engage stage and the two practice tools presented in this chapter, **The Supervision Chair** and **Placement Achievements Boxes**, go some way to enabling this. They also support the development of a safe, secure and appreciative dialogue between the practice educator and student and promote a sense of working in partnership. One practice educator who has used **The Supervision Chair** with a student said:

> *It broke down barriers really quickly. It helped to stress supervision as a joint endeavour, more equal than the usual agreement I would use... I really feel it helped us develop a fantastic working relationship.*

The student said: *'I felt really clear about my supervision and that we were working in partnership. It really helped set the scene for the type of supervision we wanted to create... It helped me understand the sort of safe space supervision could be.'*

This chapter draws heavily on therapeutic techniques. It is important to recognise that practice educators are not therapists, but we can work in a relationship-based way with students. The practice tools may indeed require the practice educator to share something of themselves. This is particularly relevant to the Social GGRRAAACCEEESSS (Burnham, 2012) discussion later in this chapter. In addition, taking a humanist perspective to adult learning, Rogers (1994) would say that congruence requires the practice educator to be true to oneself and to not be afraid to express and discuss feelings in order to develop a rapport with the learner.

For many years I have used supervision agreements with students; these have tended to cover expectations, boundaries, needs and responsibilities. I have always had conversations about power and how to make supervision a safe space too. However, these supervision agreements have always felt quite limited and formal, one-sided even. I try to model creativity, building a rapport and relationship-based practice from the start of my working relationship with students, and I began to think about how the supervision agreement was not aligned to these. When we started to work virtually at the beginning of the Covid-19 pandemic, I anticipated it was going to be even harder to develop a rapport, model creativity and 'do' relationship-based practice from the start of the practice learning opportunity. I, therefore, started to think about other ways I could carry out a supervision agreement discussion with students.

The supervision chair – What do you need to feel comfortable and secure in supervision?

Let's settle in

The Supervision Chair acts as a supervision agreement and is a visual and creative way to pay attention to the beginning of the working relationship between the practice educator and student. It has a strong focus on enabling the student to feel safe and secure, which is particularly important for virtual supervision where these elements can be more challenging.

A little theory

The Supervision Chair is influenced by the concept of a secure base, which comes originally from the work of Bowlby (1969). In line with Bowlby's concept of a secure base, supervision is seen as a comfortable chair, a safe haven to return to from the stressors of placement, where the student can safely explore feelings and thoughts, have challenging conversations to promote learning and then return to the outside world feeling that things are more manageable. Thinking about the practice educator and the student as a team, **The Supervision Chair** is also closely aligned to the concept of the team as secure base. In their model of the Team as a Secure Base, Biggart et al (2017) identify five domains for promoting a secure base: availability, sensitivity, acceptance, co-operation and membership. **The Supervision Chair** promotes these domains.

Chair legs – Availability: The practice educator is there for the student.

Chair arms and getting in and out of the chair – Sensitivity: The student feels safe enough to explore feelings.

Chair seat – Acceptance: The student's feelings, identity and views will be accepted in supervision.

Chair back and getting in and out of the chair – Co-operation: This is a joint endeavour between the practice educator and student.

Chair seat – Membership: The practice educator and student value and understand each other.

The concept of ***The Supervision Chair*** *came from thinking about my own experiences of supervision. One of my first managers, Elaine, did in fact have two comfortable armchairs in her office, which were only sat in for supervision discussions.*

I always recall feeling safe with her, in supervision, to say whatever was on my mind. When I left that chair, I often felt that I had learnt something maybe about myself or I had some new understanding to take forward. I felt more connected to my work, emotionally contained, valued and appreciated. Of course, this process was little to do with the armchair, but the way in which Elaine conducted the supervision. When I reflected on what it was Elaine actually did to enable this process to happen, availability, sensitivity, acceptance, co-operation and membership seemed to make sense.

The how-to

For working virtually, **The Supervision Chair** template can be shared with the student and used to guide the discussion. The student's comments can be written on the template as each section of the chair has been discussed. The template can be individualised by using an image of a chair chosen by the student. In comparison, when working in person, students can be asked to create a large drawing of **The Supervision Chair** or a 3D chair model with boxes and tubes. **The Supervision Chair** could also be created by using a collage of magazine pictures of chairs or online chair images. The practice educator and student can write all over the chair collage, or create speech bubbles, arrows and pictures to represent the supervision agreement discussions at each stage of building the chair.

The practice educator should start by talking to the student about the concept of supervision as a comfortable chair, a secure base. Explain that **The Supervision Chair** is built from the bottom up, similar to the concept of using co-production techniques where policy or approaches are influenced by staff or individuals.

There are six stages to building **The Supervision Chair**. The practice educator and the student talk though each stage and record the discussions, on either the template, large drawing, model or collage.

IMAGE 1.1A: 1. Chair legs – What do you need in order to feel that supervision and your supervisor are available, stable and predictable?

The practice educator may guide or prompt the student by talking about the chair needing to have four legs firmly on the ground; it needs to feel strong, like it would hold you up if you fell down; it needs to be constant, available, in the same place and the student should know how to get to the chair. Thinking of supervision in this way, what does the student need to feel that supervision and the practice educator are available, stable and predictable? Each student's responses and needs will be different, but often discussions at the chair legs stage may be connected to the following aspects of supervision:

- protected time;
- scheduled in the diary;
- in the same location;
- on time;
- knowing who will send the joining link for virtual supervision;
- who will book a room if supervision is in person;
- how long the session will last;
- what will happen if the session is cancelled;
- what your agreed supervision structure will look like;
- what preparation is expected.

All of these elements and more help **The Supervision Chair** feel stable and predictable.

IMAGE 1.1B: 2. Chair seat – What do we need to know about each other so that we can sit comfortably with each other? How can we learn more about each other? How do our values, beliefs, life and work experiences, cultural similarities and differences impact on how we 'sit' with each other? What do we need to acknowledge in terms of the seat of power and privilege? How will we sit with and manage challenge or conflict?

The practice educator may guide or prompt the student by talking about the fact that the student and the practice educator will be sitting with each other for some time. It will be important that they can feel comfortable and sit through complex discussions with some understanding of each other. This section of the chair is a good point to discuss similarities and differences and, importantly, to schedule in further plans to expand and develop these discussions. **The Supervision Chair** shouldn't be the only time the practice educator and student have these discussions. Undertaking discussions at this point of **The Supervision Chair** sets up an expectation that discussions about power, similarity and difference are part of on-going supervision.

McCaughan et al (2018) acknowledge that discussing similarities and differences at the beginning of the supervisory relationship is vital as it supports the practice educator and student to return to these discussions throughout the practice learning opportunity. Social GGRRAAACCEEESSS (Burnham, 2012) is a helpful model to assist with discussions at this point. Social GGRRAAACCEEESSS is a mnemonic to aid consideration of difference and similarity within relationships. In a linear form, it includes:

gender;

geography;

race;

religion;

age;

ability;

appearance;

class;

culture;

ethnicity;

education;

employment;

sexuality;

sexual orientation;

spirituality.

Each element can be discussed, in terms of views, experiences, similarities and differences. Consider which elements stand out to the practice educator and the student. For example, the following five questions may be helpful to consider at this point.

1. In our supervision relationship, which Social GGRRAAACCEEESSS are more visible or invisible and why?
2. Do any of our Social GGRRAAACCEEESSS provide us with more power or privilege (for example, White privilege, education or employment privilege) than the other one of us? How might this impact on our supervision relationship?
3. How might we challenge each other when we notice discrimination, bias or assumption in relation to the Social GGRRAAACCEEESSS?
4. Which of the Social GGRRAAACCEEESSS stand out to you and why do you think that is? How might that impact on supervision for you?
5. As your practice educator, is there anything you would like me to keep in mind about your Social GGRRAAACCEEESSS?

Thinking about how the student and practice educator will 'sit together comfortably' will often include some uncomfortable discussions in order to reach a comfortable point in a meaningful way. The importance of these discussions in paying attention to the early stages of the practice educator and student relationship cannot be minimised. For example, Brookfield (1995) confirms that our *cultural beliefs* are so powerful they may be more influential than our age in terms of the impact on how we learn. In addition, research by Christiansen et al (2011) also found that good supervision involved the creation of a safe space in which the supervisee could communicate and process experiences related to cultural issues.

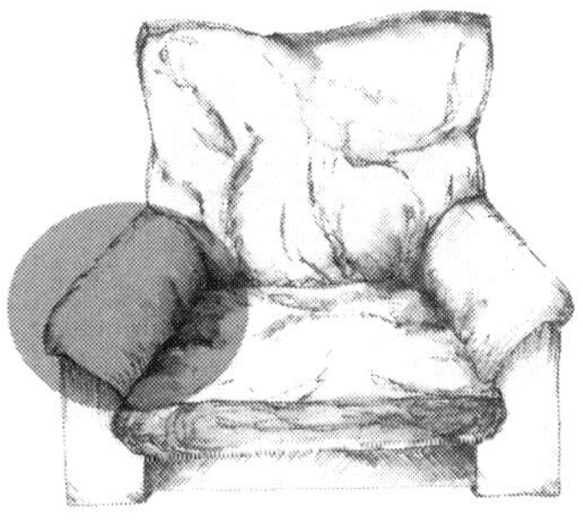

IMAGE 1.1C: 3. Chair arms – What do you need from me as a practice educator to feel accepted, emotionally contained and supported? How will you know this is happening? How might previous experiences of supervision impact on the creation of an emotionally containing supervisory relationship?

The practice educator may guide or prompt the student by talking about supervision acting as a metaphoric hug to help the student feel emotionally held, supported and accepted. The student can think about what they need from supervision in order to achieve this sense of emotional containment (Bion, 1962). A conversation about previous supervisory experiences and what helped or hindered in terms of feeling emotionally contained and supported can be helpful. Additional questions can be used such as the following.

- If feeling emotionally contained in supervision was represented in the arms of this chair...
    - » what colour would they be?
    - » how would they feel to touch?
    - » what size would they be?
    - » how would the arms feel when you sit in the chair?
- If you feel uncontained in supervision...
    - » what might I see?
    - » how will you tell me if you need your supervision chair to feel more supportive?

Each student will have different responses, but this section of the chair is an opportunity to think about what acceptance, emotional containment and support may look and feel like to them. This is increasingly important in the world of virtual supervision and can help raise self-awareness about how empathy, kindness and respect are communicated via a computer screen.

IMAGE 1.1D: 4. Chair back – What are the ground rules that will help us to stay sitting up and paying attention to each other? What learning style or thinking styles do we prefer and how will we use these? What has helped us to keep focus in previous supervisions?

The practice educator can introduce this section by encouraging the student to think about what needs to be in place in supervision so that both practice educator and student can concentrate and pay their best attention to each other. This provides a good opportunity to discuss issues such as starting on time, confidentiality, listening, turn taking, taking a comfort break and, for virtual supervision, having videos enabled. There is the opportunity here to think about learning or thinking styles and how these will be considered. Any learning from previous supervisory experiences should also be discussed, thinking about what worked well for paying attention and what hindered.

IMAGE 1.1B: 5. Getting in and out of the chair – At each supervision, what activity or ritual would help you settle into your chair at the start of supervision and to leave your chair at the end of supervision? Having left your supervision chair, how will we remember the main points from the supervision?

For this section of **The Supervision Chair**, the student may want to draw themselves standing next to the chair. At this point of **The Supervision Chair** the practice educator can talk with the student about the importance of starting and ending routines or rituals. Rituals and routines can increase a sense of safety and predictability in therapeutic work and in professional meetings such as supervision (Treisman, 2017). Students should be encouraged to think about their own starting and ending rituals for the supervision. For example, anything that starts the supervision session with a way to connect, reflect, release tension or set a nurturing tone will be helpful. This is particularly relevant with the shift towards more virtual spaces where practitioners need to find more creative ways to connect and mitigate the additional pressures virtual working creates. The practice educator may need to offer ideas or try out different techniques to find what suits the student most. This could be beginning or ending the supervision with a 'check-in' about feelings, perhaps using the question '*what does it feel like to sit in this supervision chair today?*' Other ideas may be the use of a reflective model, or a soothing technique such as a breathing exercise, or creating a **Placement Achievements Box** (see below).

This section of **The Supervision Chair** also allows for important discussions about what happens having left the chair. How will the main points from the session be remembered? Therefore, discussions around minute-taking and gathering written evidence from supervision can be undertaken.

When will we review the continued comfort of our supervision chair?

The Supervision Chair is designed to be revisited and reviewed; metaphorically, this is like plumping up or cleaning the chair cushions or checking that the chair is in the best possible position and that its legs are still firmly attached. The student may wish to draw a cushion on their supervision chair, a bottle of fabric cleaner next to the chair or a screwdriver to check the tightness of the chair legs.

In this section the practice educator and the student agree dates to formally review **The Supervision Chair** and think about any changes that may need to be made. Additional questions here which might be useful could be:

- what will we do if the chair feels uncomfortable?
- how would you let me know that the chair is not comfortable for you?

The practice educator and student may decide to have **The Supervision Chair** template, drawing, model or collage visible at each supervision as a constant reminder of what they are trying to achieve. Certainly, **The Supervision Chair** agreement should be physically present at the review stage for additional comments to be added.

*I also use **The Supervision Chair** with groups of students. For this purpose, I rename it the Student Hub Chair. We follow mostly the same prompts and discussion as **The Supervision Chair**, with just a few changes. For example, around the chair back, I add discussion about which subjects might keep the students sitting up and paying attention. We complete the Student Hub Chair on the first group session (there are usually 5–12 hub sessions for each group depending on their practice* *learning opportunity pattern). Feedback from student groups about the exercise has been positive. For example, students report that undertaking the chair helps them understand their role in helping to create a safe and yet challenging space for learning and support. Most recently at the final group student hub session, one of the students said they remembered back to the first hub session and 'doing that chair'. She continued, 'the hub has been my safe comfortable chair and the hub members have been my cushions'.*

How the tool can be utilised within social work practice

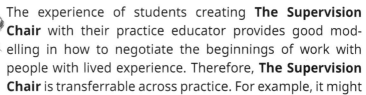

The experience of students creating **The Supervision Chair** with their practice educator provides good modelling in how to negotiate the beginnings of work with people with lived experience. Therefore, **The Supervision Chair** is transferrable across practice. For example, it might instead be called the 'visit chair' or the 'working together chair' and words or phrases could be altered to suit the situation or person. Students may find that using the chair or at least holding it in mind helps them to focus on important elements of relationship building at the start of their working relationship with families or individuals. When using **The Supervision Chair** as a working agreement between a practitioner and a family, adaptations could be used.

The Visit Chair – What do you need to feel as comfortable as possible in our work together?

Chair legs – What do you need from me to feel that our work together is stable and predictable? How will you get in touch with me? When will I see you and where?

Chair seat – What do I need to know about you or your family to help me understand you? What do I need to know about your culture, ethnicity or personal characteristics to help me understand you or your family? What do you need to help you feel as comfortable as possible in our work together? What do you need to know from me about my role?

Chair arms – How can I support you? What would that support look like? Who else might support you while you are working with me?

Chair back – What are your expectations of me? What ground rules might help us work well together?

Getting in and out of the chair – How would you like to start and end each visit? How would you like to remember the key points from each visit?

When and how will we review how comfortable the visit chair feels?

Placement achievements box

Moments of achievement

A **Placement Achievements Box** (other names can be used, such as Placement Positives Box, Placement Strengths Box, Placement Learning Box) helps to create a focus on the journey towards the ending, right from the start. Starting at the first supervision, and at each supervision throughout the practice learning opportunity, the student chooses a moment of achievement that they wish to store in their achievements box. The box is added to throughout the practice learning opportunity and kept safe by the practice educator and at the final supervision the box is given to the student.

*The **Placement Achievements Box** provides an opportunity for the student to self-evaluate. To ask, 'What have I done well this week?' I would often ask this question in supervision but recording this in the supervision notes sometimes felt like the achievement got lost among everything else. Thinking about how I could place more value on the student's achievement brought me to the idea of storing them somewhere else: a place that was purely for self-evaluation of their celebratory moments. Jars and boxes are used in many areas of therapeutic work. For example, calm boxes and sensory boxes (Treisman, 2017), and so the **Placement Achievements Box** was born.*

What makes up the box?

Placement Achievements Boxes are influenced by the strengths-based approach (Saleebey, 2012). In addition, social workers are often in the position of asking people with lived experience to describe their strengths, so in terms of experiential learning it supports students to reflect on what it feels like to be asked to identify positive aspects of themselves and their practice.

This practice tool is also influenced by the consideration of student well-being. The five ways to well-being note the importance of connection, activity, taking notice, maintaining learning and giving (Aked et al, 2014). **Placement Achievements Boxes** provide an opportunity in supervision for the practice educator and student to connect with each other and take notice of the student's successes and learning. Importantly, they provide an opportunity for the practice educator to 'give' the box to the student and for the student to give themselves the gift of self-kindness by appreciating their successes.

*An ex-student I worked with recently attended some training I was delivering for qualified workers. I had used a **Placement Achievements Box** with her when I was her practice educator, and she told me how she had continued to add to the box during her Assessed and Supported Year of Employment. Notably, she said what had been most useful about this was to take a moment out of her day to focus on an achievement, however small that was. In this way she said it had become part of her self-care routine.*

Building-a-box

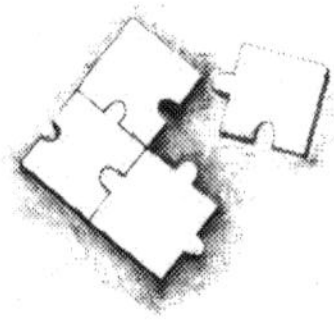

The student chooses a box at the first supervision session. They could be asked to provide the box themselves or the practice educator could provide a choice of boxes. Flat pack party boxes are cost effective, as are gift boxes, particularly if you can source a selection from charity shops! A variety of pieces of card or paper are needed; these can be different colours, shapes and sizes. The student may choose to decorate the box in a way that is personal to them.

At an agreed point in each supervision session, the practice educator asks the student to identify their 'best achievement/success' or 'special learning moment from the practice learning opportunity this week'. The practice educator or the student writes this on a chosen piece of card or paper, notes the date and adds this into the box (the names of people with lived experience should not be used). The practice educator keeps the box safe throughout the practice learning opportunity and gives the completed box to the student at the final supervision. The student can be encouraged to keep the box to add to as they move into either their next practice learning opportunity or their social work career.

The boxes can also be used by social workers and practice educators at any stage of their career. They can act as a useful reminder of success, achievements and moments of making a difference. Looking back through the box can be a helpful act of self-care, especially when things feel difficult. In the current climate of increased working at home, achievements boxes can be kept in your home workspace and added to at the end of each day; this can be a ritual to mark the end of the working day.

How the tool can be utilised within social work practice

This practice tool can be adapted in a number of ways. As an alternative to a box, a notebook could be used; this is potentially easier for the social worker to transport and keep hold of. The box or book could be referred to as the 'working together box/book' or 'memories from our work together box/book' or 'your journey box/book'. Like the student's **Placement Achievements Box,** the box or book is offered at the beginning of the work between the social worker and the person with lived experience. As with the student's box it starts the discussion at the beginning about the process of working together towards an ending. At the end of each visit the social worker asks the person what from that visit they wish to remember; this might be a standout moment, the thing they most enjoyed, a reflection or a piece of information they want to remember. Used at the end of each visit to signify the end of the visit, the box or book can be helpful for creating rituals and routines, which is especially important for increasing safety and predictability for the person. Giving the box or book to the person at the end of the working relationship acts as a way of reviewing the working together process and marking the end.

What has surprised me most when using achievement boxes or books with people with lived experience is that often the achievements or stand-out visit moment they have chosen would not have been the one I would have anticipated. It can be a humble reminder of the things that really matter to individuals.

Summary

This chapter has explored two practice tools to enhance the beginning of the student and practice educator relationship. The importance of developing a secure and safe working relationship has been stressed, but it is not enough to use a practice tool or state that a relationship 'will be safe'. Safety, predictability, trust and security must be modelled and developed over time. It is hoped that the tools support practice educators and social workers to do this from the start of the practice learning opportunity, but most importantly they require the utilisation of relational skills to provide a safe and secure base from which students or people with lived experience can grow and develop.

Three key points

1. **Power** – when using the tools described in this chapter, it cannot be ignored that whether using them with students or people with lived experience, the practice educator or social worker holds more power than the individual they are using the tool with. In addition, the context in which these tools will be used will often be an assessed situation. Hence the importance of the time spent developing the relationship from the beginning of the practice learning opportunity, where the practice educator can name the power of the assessed situation, explore how this feels and how this might be managed together.

2. **Adapt** – not all practice educators and students feel comfortable using creative methods, although I encourage you to try! If the thought of drawing a large chair on a sheet of paper or creating a special box and putting little cards or notes inside it does not resonate with you, do think about the message behind the activity and how you can adapt the activity to suit you and your student. For example, one of my practice educator colleagues and her student made a Microsoft Word document poster of the student's **Placement Achievements Moments** rather than using a box.

3. **Expand** – the practice tools and questions suggested within them are starting points for discussion; they act like a springboard for further work and discussion. There will be many ways to expand and deepen your conversations with students using curious questions and responding to what each student presents.

References

Aked, J, Marks, N, Cordon, C and Thompson, S (2014) Five Ways to Wellbeing. The New Economics Foundation Centre for Wellbeing. [online] Available at: www.neweconomics.org/projects/entry/five-ways-to-well-being (accessed 20 February 2022).

Biggart, L, Ward, E, Cook, L and Schofield, G (2017) The Team as a Secure Base: Promoting Resilience and Competence in Child and Family Social Work. *Children and Youth Services Review*, 83: 119–30.

Bion, W R (1962) *Learning from Experience*. London: Karnac Books.

Bowlby, J (1969) *Attachment and Loss, Vol. 1: Attachment.* New York: Basic Books.

Brookfield, S (1995) Adult Learning: An Overview. In Tuinjman, A (ed) *International Encyclopedia of Education* (pp 375–80). Oxford: Pergamon Press.

Burnham, J (2012) Developments in Social GRRRAAACCEEESSS: Visible-invisible and Voiced-unvoiced. In Krause, I (ed) *Culture and Reflexivity in Systemic Psychotherapy: Mutual Perspectives*. (pp 139–62). London: Karnac.

Christiansen, A T, Thomas, V, Kafescioglu, N, Karakurt, G, Lowe, W and Smith, W (2011) Multicultural Supervision: Lessons Learnt About On-going Struggle. *Journal of Marital and Family Therapy*, 37: 109–19.

Kadushin, A (1990) *The Social Work Interview*. 3rd ed. New York: Columbia University Press.

McCaughan, S, Hesk, G and Stanley, A (2018) Listening to Black Students: A Critical Review of Practice Education. In Taplin, S (ed) *Innovations in Practice Learning* (pp 101–20). St Albans: Critical Publishing.

McColgan, M and McMullin, C (eds) (2017) *Doing Relationship-based Social Work: A Practical Guide to Building Relationships and Enabling Change*. London: Jessica Kingsley Publishers.

McMullin, C (2017) Building Relationships in Social Work. In McColgan, M and McMullin, C (eds) *Doing Relationship-based Social Work: A Practical Guide to Building Relationships and Enabling Change* (pp 15–31). London: Jessica Kingsley Publishers.

Rogers, C (1994) *Freedom to Learn*. New York: Prentice Hall.

Saleebey, D (2012) *The Strengths Perspective in Social Work Practice*. 6th ed. Upper Saddle River, NJ: Pearson.

Treisman, K (2017) *A Therapeutic Treasure Box for Working with Children and Adolescents with Developmental Trauma: Creative Techniques and Activities*. London: Jessica Kingsley Publishers.

I am string

Alison Dudeney

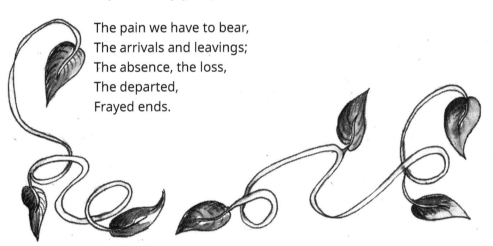

Sometimes I see myself as garden twine...
And then as grey household string,
Soft, flexible; not new,
Paired with crackling brown paper,
Almost obsolete in this age of plastic sticky tape.

I am stronger than I think.
Holding people up,
Stringing them together,
Entwining them lovingly;
Friendship is a tangled affair.

Late at night I practise threadbare knots, picking away
At loose strands, confused, disappointed sometimes,
Aching with sleeplessness.
This life, these people, those dreams.
Expectation, joy, hope.

The pain we have to bear,
The arrivals and leavings;
The absence, the loss,
The departed,
Frayed ends.

Chapter 2

Practice educating in a digital world

Anna Wright

There has been a massive shift in social work practice and for social work students, including changes to how social care is delivered, as well as how social workers interact with each other and the organisations they work for. The Covid-19 pandemic that swept the UK in early 2020 saw the government issuing stay at home orders with strict rules that leaving the home was only permissible for once-daily exercise and essential shopping and healthcare.

Overnight, a culture of office-based working and physical visits to people's homes was turned on its head. Suddenly, students were asked to stay away from the building and practice educators were left wondering how they would carry out their work, but also how they could support social work students in their practice learning opportunity. Now, a 'hybrid' model exists with students and practice educators working from home and offices. This means new and innovative ways of working are reimagined, which require practitioners to move beyond old habits and systems to embrace a new vision of learning practices.

This chapter provides you with tools to overcome some of the practical challenges of physical distance and make use of technology in a fun way so that you can support students to navigate these shifting yet intangible online environments. There is an emphasis on the consideration of the ethical and equality implications that arise as ways of working change.

*I developed the **IT Bingo** tool while working as a lead person responsible for supporting practice educators, students and Newly Qualified Social Workers in a busy London borough. We had welcomed a number of students within the practice learning opportunity with more due to begin. The outbreak of Covid-19 meant that everyone had to get used to the previously unopened application on their computers, Microsoft Teams. It quickly became clear that inductions needed to take place remotely and that among the challenges to be overcome was a huge range of ability in accessing and using technology. I needed to find a way to let people explore the technology and to get to grips with the tools as well as get to know other new starters and students without putting more pressure on busy* *practice educators. Lots of the early induction tasks were individual or procedural tasks so I wanted to create something that had the potential for a social aspect as well as increasing student confidence and highlighting any access issues.*

Eyes down...

The induction period can feel intense for practice educators and the teams around them, while students often report feeling that they have times where they are not sure what they should be doing with their time and may not have built links within the teams in order to be able to make full use of the opportunities to shadow colleagues. Spending more time working remotely might mean that students have fewer opportunities to see how other people use technology to its fullest potential or do not know how to fix problems when they arise.

The **IT Bingo** tool can be used as a planned activity that practice educators can give to an individual or group of students and then follow up in supervision. It can be used as an initial self-assessment and be revisited and updated throughout the practice learning opportunity to track developments towards the student's agreed end goal.

IT Bingo to develop technical confidence

Make a video call	Invite someone into a call	Set up an email signature	Turn out of office on and off
Set a reminder on your calendar	Create a Microsoft Teams meeting and invite someone to it	Create a mailing list with the people in your team in it	Set up a recurring item on your calendar
Delete an item from your calendar	Recall an email	Look up someone in the organisation's directory	Create a questionnaire in Microsoft Forms
Send a calendar invite	Raise your hand in a meeting	Send a message to everyone in a meeting	Send a message to an individual
Share your screen with someone	Create a Word document and save it on OneDrive	Work on a shared document at the same time as someone	Start a virtual white-board in a meeting and get someone else to draw on it

Make a video call	Invite someone into a call	Set up an email signature	Turn out of office on and off
Turn your video on and off	Mute and unmute yourself	Change your background	Change your photo in your profile
Complete the mandatory training module on...	Find the emergency contact list in the shared drive and add your details	Create an Excel spreadsheet	Collaborate with someone to create a picture. Screenshot this and send to your practice educator to finish the bingo board!

Knock at the Door, Number Four

Practice educators need to be confident with technology in their own professional practice and as educators teach and assess students within the digital practice environment. The European Framework for the Digital Competence of Educators (Redecker, 2017) explores how educators can plan learning opportunities that combine teaching, guidance, collaborative learning and self-regulated learning so students develop the skills they need to communicate, problem solve and use technology responsibly in a professional context. They may need support to develop digital capabilities that are very different to their personal use to empower and advocate for the people they support.

Students will begin their practice learning opportunity with a range of backgrounds and experiences. For example, there may be an assumption that students are tech savvy and even that they might know more than experienced workers. However, while younger people are more likely to use the internet on a regular basis and the 'digital divide' is narrowing, there remain stark differences depending on factors such as geography, economic and employment status, ethnicity and disability (ONS, 2019).

Singh (2020) highlights that campus-based learning provides an equal environment for students where internet access is freely available, where lack of access to these spaces will impact most on less privileged students. Practice educators will need to consider how students are affected practically and financially when required to work from home on a regular basis. Some may require a different response from you or a conversation between you, the practice learning organisation and the course provider.

Practice educators will need to be able to plan learning opportunities and assessments which can support students to achieve key competencies while allowing room for individual students to progress at different speeds and follow their interests, whether that is through developing communication skills in online spaces, problem solving and enhancing the use of technology in their practice or exploring the ethics of digital practice (Redecker, 2017).

Bingo dabbers at the ready!

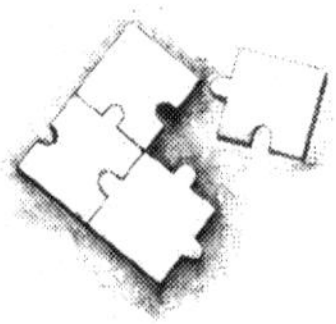

With individual students

1. Use the **IT Bingo** tool as a self-assessment task before supervision. Share the grid with the student and ask them to colour in any sections which they know they can do. While you are doing supervision online, you can ask them to demonstrate using the function described in the bingo table.
2. Agree which functions they think they can go away and try out on their own or with a peer and assign these sections a colour too.
3. Finally, identify which skills they need some additional guidance or training to do and make a plan for how this will be met, and record this in your supervision notes.
4. At future supervisions review the progress that has been made until all sections are achieved.

With groups

1. Identify a group of people who are starting in the organisation at a similar time. You may need to collaborate with other practice educators or the workforce development lead to achieve this.
2. Introduce the group to the bingo board and ask them to work together to complete the tasks in pairs or small groups. You could use a group chat function in order for them to have space to ask each other questions and to agree time to work things out together. You may want to allocate them some time to work together on this initially.

3. You could award a small prize to the group who are able to colour in all of the squares and complete the task in the starred box first.

Several social work students were joining an organisation over a particular month. The practice educators working alongside these students created a fixed point within the first month of starting for the students to meet online and complete the ***IT Bingo*** *tool. Students were able to help each other to try out functionality and enjoyed time informally together without 'educators' present to get to know each other and talk about their practice learning experiences so far. Those students who had not received all of their equipment or training met at the office to share with peers or use desktop computers so that they could still take part in the activity.*

The practice educators made this a monthly event where students could hear from guest speakers or do group work on themes suggested by the student group which allowed them to continue to learn collaboratively.

How this tool can be used in social work practice

Many more social work visits and meetings have taken place online. It is crucial that social workers are confident in the use of technology in order to share this with people who they support, so that they have a voice when decisions are being made and so that they are supported in a way that best meets their needs and preferences. The **IT Bingo** tool could be adapted in a number of ways, such as the following.

- For use with groups or individuals to prepare for taking part in meetings and checking which functions of the system they don't have access to or prefer to use. For example, if joining as a guest they might not be able to see or read the chat so the meeting format might need to be adapted so they are not disadvantaged. Or they might know that they would prefer to have their camera off because of their internet connection and want support to explain that at the beginning.
- Students could work with the people they support to review the bingo tool to see if there are skills that they think their worker would need.
- It could be used with family and professional carers to ensure they have the skills to help the people they support to stay in touch with their family, friends and professional network.

Scaling tool to discuss working from home

Working online is unhelpful for this aspect of my learning and social work practice. 	<------------------------>	This factor of my learning and social work practice is enhanced by working online. 

Working online from home has been a shift over the last year but it is here to stay! Working in this way has pros and cons and I hear from experienced workers who are able to think about what they gain or lose from being online. They can take notice of what is missing, which helps them make decisions about how they structure their work and home lives to maintain their well-being and work effectively.

However, students are still developing a professional identity and may not have a full toolkit in relation to self-care. The power relationships between students and the organisation may mean they feel less confident or enabled to make decisions about how and where they 'do' social work. Some practice educators may find it hard to identify or advocate for their student's needs, especially where the student has not been able to articulate themselves, or are operating within the context of a tricky organisational system.

Introduction

The **Scaling** tool is designed as a way to enable conversations between students and practice educators about different aspects of online working, whether it is working from home arrangements or carrying out assessments and having conversations online. Of course, there are no right answers, but the responses from students may identify differences in expectations and assumptions that require discussion, such as: how often is 'healthy'

or 'desirable' to work from home? What is optimal for the student's learning? And what is beneficial for supporting people with lived experience to have 'a voice' within decision making about them or their family member?

There are ethical, practical and professional tensions in relation to some use of technology in social work practice and this is recognised in the BASW (2020) Digital Capabilities Statement, which has been produced to supplement the Professional Capabilities Framework (BASW, 2018). Taylor-Beswick (2021) argues that there needs to be more critical thought about how to align social work values with digital practice so that people are not marginalised and so that there can be increased assurance that the digital tools and methods used for social work practice are ethically sound. The **Scaling** tool seeks to introduce some of these ideas for further discussion.

Theory

Undertaking a social work practice learning opportunity while responding to a pandemic and working from home has impacted students' finances, well-being and health in myriad ways (Hitchcock et al, 2021; Lange and Maynard, 2021). Practice educators will likely be cognisant of some of these from their own experience or that of their peers. However, when supporting students, it is important that they are particularly mindful of aspects of identity and diversity, which have been linked to increased experiences of alienation from work and student life. In contrast, for others the opposite may be true, where working from home may have offered some relief from personal or environmental stressors (Lorimer et al, 2021; Unison, 2020).

Considering disabled workers as an example, a survey of 4455 disabled people working in the public sector by Unison (2020) found that 74 per cent of disabled people who worked at home during the Covid-19 pandemic felt they were more or as productive as when they were based in the workplace. Reasons such as flexibility in start times, ability to take regular breaks and reduced requirement to commute were given. However, it is important to remember that no group is homogenous; 27 per cent of people felt they were less productive and only half (54 per cent) felt it would be beneficial to work from home in future. Some negative impacts were common to non-disabled colleagues such as childcare pressures and lack of suitable workspace. Others were specific to disability, such as a lack of accessible communication systems or an absence of reasonable adjustments, factors which in turn impacted on mental health. This highlights the importance of having conversations with students about their experiences so that barriers can be identified and dismantled.

Even outside of the pandemic, social work involves working with people in distressed and distressing situations. Hitchcock et al (2021) suggest that trauma-informed teaching practices are important for supporting social work students who are contending simultaneously with personal and community-based traumas (see Chapter 4). Central to this approach are principles of trust and transparency and the creation of structure to help navigate periods of turbulence. Self-efficacy and motivation can be promoted through offering flexibility and choices where possible, such as in the way that particular aspects of student capability are assessed. Well-being can be supported through support, connectivity, mutuality and collaboration with others; this can be created through opportunities to meet and work with other students and to have informal social time.

How to use the tool

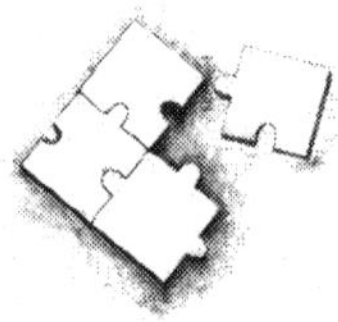

If you are working with a student online, present the **Scaling** tool on the screen in a way that you and your student can draw on it, such as the whiteboard application on Microsoft Office or via Zoom.

The words and phrases are split into four sections so that the conversation can be focused or move between thinking of the pros and cons for the student, the practice learning and practice educator, people who the student will be working with and the team or organisation.

Share with them a list of the words and phrases and ask them to choose where they would place each statement along the continuum.

You may want to discuss these one at a time or go through a range and then see which factors require addressing.

Other ways

You could use the **Scaling** tool as a group activity. You may also want to add to the words and phrases or remove some in order to have a more detailed conversation about a particular aspect of practice.

Words and phrases

My individual factors	*My learning and support needs*
Balancing caring responsibilities	*Being supported by my practice educator*
Travel time	*Accessing training*
Looking after my physical self	*Being able to complete direct observations*
Having good routines	*Getting feedback from people who I have supported or worked with*
Balancing screen time	*Connecting with other students*
Sharing space with my family	*Having opportunities to shadow other workers*
Having quiet space to work	*Having reflective supervision*
Having an accessible workspace	*Having a range of opportunities*
Being motivated and engaged	*Knowing whether I am doing a good job*
Recovering from stressful situations	*Meeting the PCF standards*
Knowing it is time to take a break	*Being able to try things out and make mistakes*
Personal finances and access to funds for work-related expenses	*Having time to read and reflect*
Having social contact	*Linking theory to practice*
Finishing work and having a home life	
Being able to worship and celebrate important occasions	

→

My life in the team and organisation	***My ability to practise effectively***
Accessing stable internet and workplace resources	*Managing my workload*
Being able to contact people for support	*Building relationships*
Being included	*Doing direct work with people*
Knowing who everyone is	*Helping people access the services they need*
Knowing who to go to if I need help or if I've made a mistake	*Making accurate assessments*
Understanding the organisational values and priorities	*Involving people who might be excluded*
Keeping sensitive data safe and secure	*Ensuring people have a voice in decisions and meetings*
Seeing people 'like me' in the team or organisation, eg people of a similar age, gender, culture, religion, ethnicity or who are LGBT+	*Assessing housing conditions and the quality of relationships*
Managing my personal vs professional online presence	*Helping people when they are distressed*
	Treating people equally and fairly
	Using technology ethically
	Understanding people's cultural heritage
	Supporting people in the way that they choose

Kojo's student, Maria, produced high-quality work and was well liked by the team, but he noticed that she often sent work through quite late in the evening and he was worried about the hours that she was keeping in order to do her work. The team were under a lot of pressure and many people struggled to keep a work–life balance at times. He was really keen for Maria to learn good habits so that she would develop as a resilient social worker!

Kojo asked Maria to cut out the phrases ready for supervision, to give her the opportunity to think through some of the areas. Kojo planned to discuss 'finishing work and having a home life' but decided to let Maria lead the conversations with the areas she felt strongest about. Through this conversation Maria was able to share that on the days that she worked from home she would rate highly 'balancing caring responsibilities' and 'looking after my physical self' as she was able to see her children to school and complete the physical therapy she needs because of her disability. She explained she would work later on those days, after her children had gone to bed, which is why she often sent emails late. She was most worried that working from home a lot was impacting on 'having opportunities to shadow other workers' as she had not been invited to join any virtual visits.

Maria was glad to have been able to speak openly about how she was managing her time and Kojo was reassured that she was not working overtime. They discussed how to balance out the week and how Maria could communicate her plans with him at the start of each week. They let her academic tutor and the team manager know what they had agreed; Kojo approached a few people in the team to firm up plans for shadowing and they discussed in a team meeting about how technology formats could be ethically used to achieve this once consent had been obtained.

How this tool can be used in social work practice

You or your student could use the **Scaling** tool to enable a discussion with an individual about how they receive support from social workers and access services online compared to visiting an office or having home visits. Encourage the student to consider what phrases they might want to make available to do the activity. This will require them to empathise with the needs and perspectives of a range of people, critically reflect about social work relationships and consider risk assessment as part of online social work practice. This would be particularly beneficial at an early stage within the practice learning opportunity as it gives an opportunity for relationship building and for the student to adapt their practice based on the feedback. Perhaps there may be some key messages for the team or organisation which may also emerge.

A team checklist for creating a learning team culture in the context of remote working

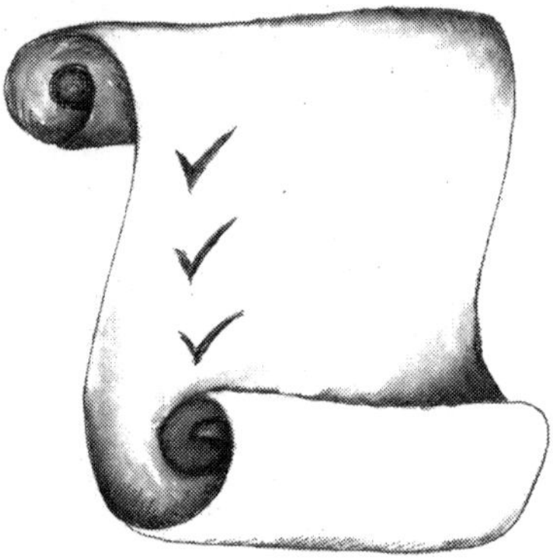

Preparing for a student to join you is an important aspect of your role as practice educators, whether that be ensuring that the team is on board, personally feeling ready and making space for the student or informing people with lived experience about the new starter. I supported a student in somewhat ideal circumstances, as an established worker in a stable and supportive team with an encouraging manager. Most colleagues were mindful of what a student might need from us and were enthusiastic about working with them and we had an office base that was 'ours' which most people came to on most days. Despite this, there were still some challenges that I didn't foresee and that we had to work out as we went along.

Over the years, in my various roles as off-site practice educator, university-based tutor and from within a learning and development team, I have supported numerous students and teams where the context is more challenging; teams may be in a state of flux or be understaffed, and colleagues may not understand the role of the student or their own role in shaping their learning. Remote working can exacerbate some of these challenges and lead to situations where practice educators or students feel isolated or overwhelmed. This tool has been developed to support you as a practice educator to begin a conversation within your team about how you will best support a student as a team and how barriers due to remote working can be addressed.

Introduction

The **Team Checklist** tool identifies what practice educators and teams will need to think about when preparing to welcome a student.

You can use the **Team Checklist** tool before you have a student join the team to discuss things with your colleagues and set expectations. For students who are on their first practice learning opportunity, or if you are working with an on-site supervisor and off-site practice educator model, you may find this checklist helpful as part of the preparations for the learning agreement meeting. You could return to this plan if there have been changes in the team or if things are not going smoothly to review what aspects of support are in place and what needs to be developed to support the student holistically.

Theory

The Team as Secure Base Model (Biggart et al, 2017) (Figure 2.1) is based on attachment theory and considers that individuals will be able to function optimally, confidently and creatively and be most resilient to stress when the team is able to function as an emotionally secure base. A secure base is provided when the five aspects of availability, sensitivity, acceptance, co-operation and membership are modelled. Individual supervision is crucial for this but so is the culture and behaviour of the wider team.

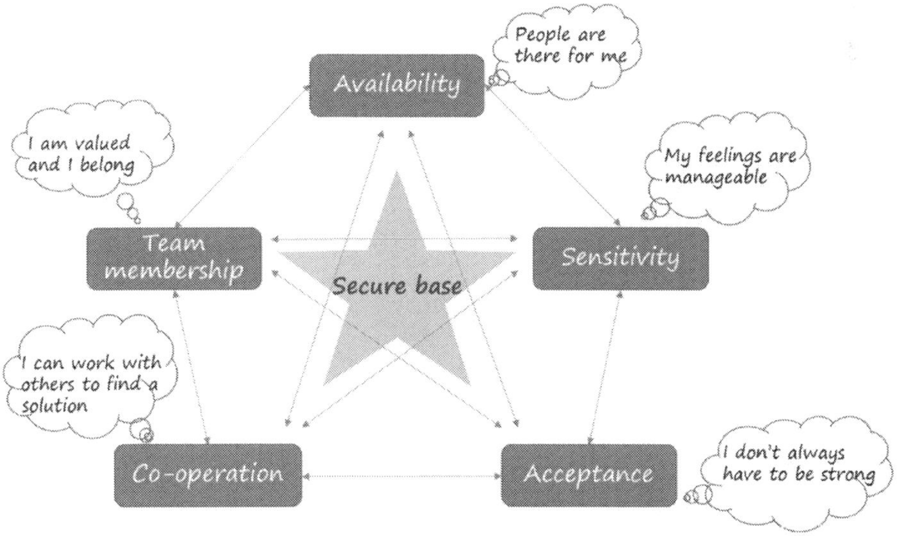

Figure 2.1 The Secure Base Model for teams
(Biggart et al, 2017)

Cook et al (2020) interviewed 31 child and family social workers at the beginning of the pandemic during the first 12 weeks of lockdown. They found that it was possible for the team to function as a secure base during a time of remote working. However, some aspects may be more challenging and these require practice educators and team managers to consider what extra things may need to happen for students, new starters and those who are on the 'outside' of the team dynamics. Cook et al (2020) found that it can be harder to benefit from team membership where there are no opportunities for informal 'water cooler' conversations; social media or team communication channels that might create a sense of **availability** for an established team member might exacerbate feelings of exclusion for others. People who may not be so well integrated into the team or who are not vocal when feeling under pressure may miss out on the **sensitivity** of the team that could help them feel better able to manage their emotions.

It is the practice educator's role to shape the learning environment for the student and build understanding of the roles and expectations of all involved in supporting and assessing that learning (BASW, 2019). In the examples above, the practice educator may want to introduce a discussion in supervision or a team meeting about the unspoken rules that determine social media use, or they could identify a 'buddy' to have a regular check-in with the student to allow space to air any concerns or stresses. Establishing these roles and responsibilities and making them explicit is beneficial because where there is structure in place and if students understand where they can go for support, they will experience increased self-efficacy (Hitchcock et al, 2021).

In summary, the **Team Checklist** tool is underpinned by the Team as a Secure Base with consideration of good practice in student support.

Joining the team (team membership)	Team Plan
What would team members like to contribute to the plan for the student's induction period?	
When will the student meet each team member?	
What is it important for the student to see in practice? When? How will shadowing opportunities be offered and arranged? What steps need to be taken to gain consent?	

Who will the student be welcomed by on their first day?	
Which team member can act as a team buddy, eg on the days that the practice educator cannot be available?	
How will work be identified so that it fits with the student's learning needs? Who will allocate work?	
How can the team ask the student to help with specific tasks?	
Will the student take part in the duty rota? Who will support them with this?	
Availability	
How do the team contact each other a) in an emergency, b) with a non-urgent query, or c) if they need a debrief? What are the spoken and unspoken rules about who to contact or how?	
How will the team know where and when the student will be working? How will the student know who works on what days?	
How will the student know who is in their team when they come to the office if they have only met online before?	
Which group emails, discussion forums and calendar invites should the student be added to? Who will do this?	
Who can offer support with any technology glitches?	
How can the student be included in early days when they might not have access to the work-place systems such as email and video calling?	

→

Connecting for practice (co-operation)	
How will team members tell and teach the student about their roles and areas of special interest?	
What do team members hope a student will bring to the team?	
How will the student be introduced to other key people who they might need support from such as area managers or partner teams?	
Where else will students be on placement and what opportunities will there be for them to be put in touch; provide peer support or work together?	
What staff networks are available to the student and how will they be told about them? (eg LBGTQ+ network, learning and development opportunities, reading groups)	
How do the team share and talk about research and theory? Is there anything different they would like to do to support the student?	
What knowledge would the team like the student to help them update?	
Will the student have access to all of the training that the team do?	
Sensitivity	
Do the team have regular check-ins? What is the purpose and content of these? (eg service updates or informal discussion or both?)	
Who will check in with the student each day?	
How is work–life balance discussed and modelled in the team?	
Do students in your service have access to workplace counselling? Do you know what services are available to them from the university?	

How will the student's case supervision be recorded and how will they contribute to supervision discussions with allocated workers?	
What will team members do if they are concerned about the student's wellbeing?	
Acceptance	
How is difference recognised and celebrated in the team? How does the team share opinions and experiences?	
What are the different ways in which people express themselves in the team? Are any dominant in the team culture? How will the team adapt to include the student?	
How are successes celebrated in the team? How will team members give feedback to the student and practice educator about things they have done well?	
How can the team support the student to reflect on responses and feedback from individuals so that it shapes their learning and practice?	
Do the team know how to give feedback for the student in a way that can be incorporated into the practice educator's assessment and included in their portfolio?	
Who should the student contact if they are worried about something they have seen/heard or done?	
How are mistakes discussed and learned from in the team? Is there anything new or different in how this is managed for the student?	
At what point should the practice educator be told about concerns about the student's practice?	
Actions Required:	

How to use the tool

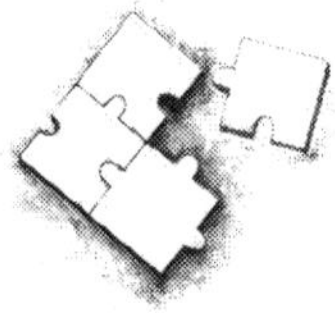

You can use the **Team Checklist** tool on your own to support your thinking first and then introduce to the team, or share it with the team from the outset. There is a column to detail the team's planned response to particular areas of support for the student.

Some aspects may require decision making from a manager, discussion with the student or clarification of expectations from the course provider; these can be recorded in the action plan section at the end to be followed up and brought back for review.

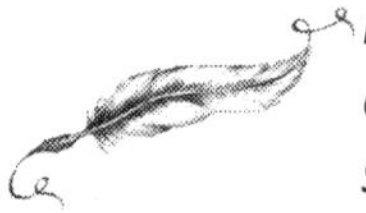

Philippa, a practice educator, has just joined a team and is expecting a student to begin a practice learning opportunity soon. Philippa has been very busy getting to know the people that she is supporting and has had less opportunity to know the team, especially as she is part time. Philippa has heard that the last student in that team had a poor experience, but this hasn't been the perspective of the team or manager.

*Philippa shared the **Team Checklist** tool with her team and found it really useful. They didn't discuss every question in detail, but it started helpful conversations. Some team members said they hadn't fully appreciated all of the thought that has to go into supporting a student. One team member said they would like to be a buddy for the student and would make sure they checked in on the days that Philippa doesn't work. The team discussed in some detail the kinds of work that they could ask the student to help with, and they realised that there had not been a clear idea of whether the work was right for the previous student's learning needs, who had become overwhelmed with the volume of conflicting demands from different workers. They agreed that this time they would propose work to Philippa and that she would discuss with the team manager if this was an appropriate piece of work. Everyone agreed this would be fairer for the student and that it would be more beneficial to the team if each team member had the same opportunity to co-work in this way.*

*Philippa has found that the team are quite loud and boisterous, and so she finds it quite hard to be part of general discussions. The **Team Checklist** tool helped her lead a conversation in a more structured way with the team. She will review the team plan towards the end of the student's practice learning opportunity and plans to spend some time asking the team to reflect on the question about how the team express themselves (acceptance) and what this means for newcomers to the team.*

How this tool can be used in social work practice

Ask the student to review the checklist and team plan and see whether there is anything that they would add for future students. They could bring this to life for future students or for individuals by creating team 'Pen Pictures'. This could include a photo or drawing of the team member and what their areas of specialism and expertise are. This could include best ways to contact and working patterns. Team members could use these to introduce themselves at case transfer or to be more inclusive in multi-agency meetings involving people with lived experience.

A 'Pen Picture for the team' could say what the remit of the team is but also what they are proud of, with pages added for other key people including administrators, managers and other key decision makers.

Three key points

1. The Covid-19 pandemic has pushed practice out of the office and community and, perhaps reluctantly, into an online space. Live social work is now happening and being transmitted directly into social workers' and students' homes. The blurring of boundaries between private and professional space will create greater anxiety and barriers to education for some students than for other or for employed staff. Welcoming a student to the team can serve as a moment to pause and consider the ethical and practical implications of online working and contribute to conversations about what the 'new normal' of hybrid, online and in-person working should look like.

2. Relationships and trauma-informed approaches should be central to practice education so that students are supported in a way that understands and mediates anxieties, and also honours the diverse perspectives of students. This is important for student well-being and ensuring individuals receive high-quality, consistent social work input that is enriched by the wealth of experiences that students bring to their practice (see Chapter 4).

3. Working online offers lots of opportunities! With the creativity and commitment that is inherent to social work, positive learning environments can be enabled. By modelling this as educators we enable students to work thoughtfully and creatively to include people with lived experience in the discussions and decisions that are made about them and their community.

References

Biggart, L, Ward, E, Cook, L and Schofield, G (2017) The Team as a Secure Base: Promoting Resilience and Competence in Child and Family Social Work. *Children and Youth Services Review*, 83: 119–30.

British Association of Social Workers (BASW) (2018) Professional Capabilities Framework. [online] Available at: www.basw.co.uk/social-work-training/professional-capabilities-framework-pcf (accessed 20 February 2022).

British Association of Social Workers (BASW) (2019) *BASW England Practice Educator Professional Standards for Social Work*. [online] Available at: www.basw.co.uk/system/files/resources/peps-for-social-work.pdf (accessed 20 February 2022).

British Association of Social Workers (BASW) (2020) Digital Capabilities Statement for Social Workers. [online] Available at: www.basw.co.uk/digital-capabilities-statement-social-workers (accessed 20 February 2022).

Cook, L, Zschomler, D, Biggart, L and Carder, S (2020) The Team as Secure Base Revisited: Remote Working and Resilience Among Child and Family Social Workers During COVID-19. *Journal of Children's Services*, 15(4).

Hitchcock, L, Creswell Báez, J, Sage, M, Marquart, M, Lewis, K and Smyth, N (2021) Social Work Educators' Opportunities During COVID-19: A Roadmap for Trauma-Informed Teaching During Crisis. *Journal of Social Work Education*, 57: 82–98.

Lange, C and Maynard, R (2021) Embracing 'Un'-certainty in Practice Education. In Turner, D (ed) *Social Work and Covid 19: Lessons for Education and Practice* (pp 43–51). St Albans: Critical Publishing.

Lorimer, A, Sentamu, F and Sharples, R (2021) From Surviving to Thriving: The Experience of Social Work Students and Their Families in Lockdown. In Turner, D (ed) *Social Work and Covid-19: Lessons for Education and Practice* (pp 53–62). St Albans: Critical Publishing.

Office for National Statistics (ONS) (2019) Exploring the UK's Digital Divide. [online] Available at: www.ons.gov.uk/peoplepopulationandcommunity/householdcharacteristics/homeinternetandsocialmediausage/articles/exploringtheuksdigitaldivide/2019-03-04#toc (accessed 20 February 2022).

Redecker, C (2017) *European Framework for the Digital Competence of Educators*. Luxembourg: Publications Office of the European Union. [online] Available at: https://publications.jrc.ec.europa.eu/repository/handle/JRC107466 (accessed 20 February 2022).

Singh, G (2020) Supporting Black, Asian Minority Ethnic (BAME) Students During the Covid-19 Crisis. [online] Available at: https://shadesofnoir.org.uk/supporting-black-asian-minority-ethnic-bame-students-during-the-covid-19-crisis (accessed 20 February 2022).

Taylor-Beswick, A (2021) Social Work, Technologies and Covid-19. In Turner, D (ed) *Social Work and Covid 19: Lessons for Education and Practice* (pp 7–13). St Albans: Critical Publishing.

Unison (2020) Covid-19 and Disabled Workers: Time for a Home Working Revolution. [online] Available at: www.unison.org.uk/content/uploads/2020/08/Covid19-and-disabled-workers-Time-for-a-home-working-revolution.docx (accessed 20 February 2022).

Chapter 3

Anti-racist social work practice education

Garfield Hunt

Introduction

The word 'racism' is unpalatable to some people; however, it is widespread, pervasive and very much part of the UK's history. While individuals might not want to be 'tarred with the racism brush', their attitude, behaviour, bigotry and, at times, outright blatantly offensive language, both written and verbal, suggests that racism is endemic within the UK in the 21st century. Institutional racism and discrimination cannot exist alone; it permeates family units, the workplace (large and small organisations), educational establishments and society as a whole due to individuals holding prejudicial thoughts in the first instance. If this goes 'unchecked' as it were, then it is possible to see how these personal views become culturally acceptable through small group acceptance of the negative stereotypes of 'others' at home and in the workspace. That culture can then seep into institutions we work in and receive our services from, moving it beyond the fallacy of 'a few bad apples' to something much more entrenched. Put simply, should those personal prejudices have been allowed to become subconsciously 'acceptable', then it should be of no surprise that the very structures that we rely on are themselves institutionally racist (Thompson, 2021).

When contemplating anti-racism, some individuals might indicate that they are 'non-racist'. This stance could be regarded as somewhat 'wishy-washy' in social work practice and education: these individuals may not have racist thoughts or ideology, but would not necessarily challenge or question racist language or behaviour if they observed it. Social work practice and education requires an 'anti' (active), as opposed to a passive ('non'), stance if social justice is realistically to be brought about (Kendi, 2020). Anti-racist social work practice requires the individual to 'do' something. At a lower level, this might involve a gentle challenge, a question as to why the individual thinks that way and/or where those ideas might originate from, and at a more direct level, to report inappropriate behaviour to management or make a formal complaint.

This chapter will provide three simple but highly effective tools for practice educators to utilise when working with social work students, apprentices and Newly Qualified Social Workers (NQSWs). Given the amount of press accorded to racism and racist incidents both in the UK and abroad, students need to equip themselves with the skills, knowledge and practice tools to enable them to be the most effective social work practitioners they can be. A belief that racism 'doesn't happen in the UK', 'not in my town/village' or 'that doesn't concern me because everyone I work with will probably be white' would be concerning; however, anecdotal evidence suggests that this is often heard on social work programmes in areas where there is a lack of ethnic diversity. To quote Nelson Mandela (1990, cited in The British Psychological Society, 2020) '*Education is the most powerful weapon which you use to change the world*'. Let us all be a part of that weapon.

'Ch-ch-ch-changes'

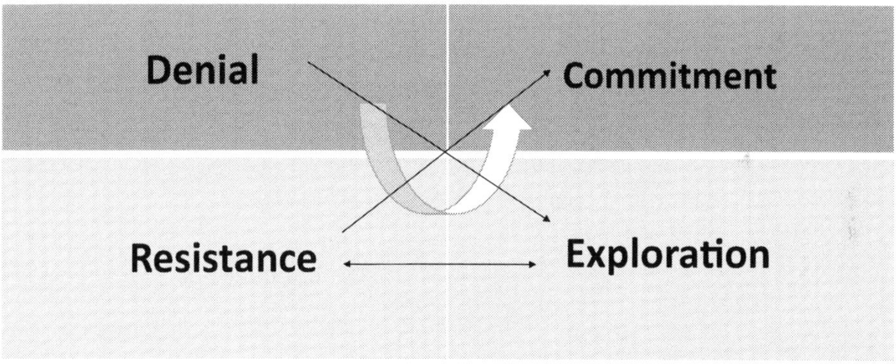

I was a social work student in the mid-nineties when I was introduced to a model by one of my lecturers. In terms of my own personal and critical reflection, it had a profound and long-lasting effect on how I viewed discrimination and how the model could be applied to all forms of discrimination – not just racism. For example, this model helped me to consider my views of same-sex relationships. The process of reflection enabled me to contemplate my own experiences of personal, cultural and institutional racism and the impact this had on me, and I began to question my attitude and its origins, which for me was a 'lightbulb' moment. As will be explained through application of this model, I quickly moved from the point of denial to commitment and have not looked back since.

Origins

The **Ch-ch-ch-changes Model** draws on Elizabeth Kübler-Ross' (1969) 'change curve' model, related to death, grief and loss, but has been adapted over the years to suit a number of audiences (eg leadership, business, coaching and career change). The model has adapted Scott and Jaffe's (1988) 'change grid' which was primarily used for the purposes of management, leadership and development; however, it is easily transferable to social work practice to consider change in personal and professional values. The model can also be mapped closely with Festinger's (1957) theory of *cognitive dissonance* (see the example questions to see the cross-correlation between the change grid and Festinger's theory).

The model can be used as an effective tool in supervision for practice educators with students wishing to explore their position and attitude towards various forms of discrimination, but for the purpose of this chapter, there is a focus on 'race' and racism. As a process, it will support not only the student to be (critically) reflective, but the practice educator too. It will aid practice educators and students alike to consider whether their position in relation to racism is 'passive' (eg 'non-racist') or is in fact linked to activism and social justice ('anti'). However, practice educators do not need to possess specialist knowledge in relation to anti-racist practice in order to undertake this activity with students.

Theory

Kübler-Ross' (1969) model helps us to recognise that responses to loss and change are not static, and helpfully demonstrates how individuals cope and resolve potentially painful experiences through various stages. Scott and Jaffe's (1988) adaptation of Kübler-Ross' model suggests that change is a step-by-step process. Although we might accept this on one level, we also need to accept that while change *can* be sequential, Stroebe and Schut (2010) propose that it can also 'oscillate' between loss (ie grief oriented) and restoration (ie goal oriented), and my proposed adaptation of the change curve would support this (see **Ch-ch-ch-changes Model**). That is to say, an individual might start in denial, move to exploration, but as a consequence of an impactful experience return to either resistance or denial. If we can appreciate that change is not predictable, sequential or static, the model can be utilised more effectively.

How does it work?

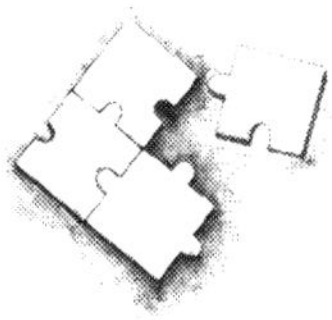

During student supervision, practice educators might discuss racism in general, or a racial incident in the local/national news, the community or on placement. The model could be applied in relation to the student's positioning on the matter, and/or to discuss feelings about the nation's perspective on the subject. The four areas of the quadrant can be explored sequentially or can relate directly to the practice educator's perception of the student's responses. Remember, the student could well be in the '*exploration*' quadrant *before* the supervision session – so try to avoid making assumptions; however, the 'shock' of the incident might have returned them to *denial* or *resistance*.

Example questions (by no means exhaustive) to be asked by the practice educator (PE) include the following.

1. **Denial/Unconscious Incompetence.** Festinger suggests: we don't know what we don't know (blissful ignorance).

PE exploration – '*What is your viewpoint and understanding/interpretation of what has happened?*' (the initial response will help you to consider step 2 and so on. For example, if denial is evident, you will need to stay here and examine further).

2. **Resistance/Conscious Incompetence.** Festinger suggests: we start to become aware of what we don't know, but that knowledge is too painful; therefore, it is suppressed. This is the most difficult and unpleasant stage of the process. Consequently, we are more likely to revert to denial as it is more comfortable.

PE exploration – '*How do you feel about the incident?*', '*When did you first become aware of racial difference?*', '*How did/does it make you feel?*', '*In terms of diversity, what did your school friendship circles look like?*', '*What, if any, were the discussions around "race" and diversity like in your family growing up?*', '*If you wanted to explore such matters in your family, how did it feel?*', '*Who were you comfortable discussing it with (if anyone)?*'

3. **Exploration/Conscious Competence.** Festinger suggests: we become aware of what we have learnt and are keen to 'get it right'.

PE exploration – *'Why do you think you are at this stage?', 'What do you think you have learned up until now?', 'How will you know that you have not slipped back into denial or resistance?', 'What actions do think you need to take now?'*

4. **Commitment/Unconscious Competence.** Festinger suggests: we are so confident and committed to the task that we go into 'automatic pilot'.

PE exploration – *'What part do you think you have to play in anti-racism?', 'What will you do (realistically) to help to reduce the impact of racism?', 'How might this be achievable?', 'How will you* know *if this has been helpful and/or achieved?'*

When I was in practice, I used this model with social work students I supervised and was practice educator for on placement. Invariably, and for a variety of reasons, I found that students tended not to think about or consider the impact and effects of racism (all the students placed with me were white/British/female). It was only when a newsworthy event was covered in the news did such discussions take place.

Having undertaken the role of practice educator previously, on one occasion, during a student supervision meeting with 'Tasha', a young, white female, she explained that the topic of race and racism had been raised during a teaching session at her university. Tasha's view of what turned out to be an unprovoked attack on a young black man in Birmingham was that 'racism doesn't really happen in Britain anymore'.

This statement immediately suggested to me that Tasha was in denial; therefore, a full discussion around the origins and impact of racism in the UK ensued with application of the adapted model and impactful questions. This resulted in Tasha's view shifting from denial to resistance and back to resistance. From a strengths perspective, and after a single supervision session, I considered this as progress. At completion of the placement, Tasha remarked that the model had helped her to explore her personal prejudices deeper and was determined to be more open to enquiring into her originally held values.

It should be remarked here that there is no assumption that the practice educator possesses the confidence and skills in tackling matters around this subject. You do not have to be a specialist on the subject in any way; however, as a starting point, it could be a helpful tool for opening up initial conversations with students.

How the tool can be utilised within social work practice

The model can be used effectively for purposes of critical reflection by individuals, in supervision or in groups. People with lived experience may well also find this a valuable model; however, *this would be dependent on their willingness to be open to self-reflection and constructive feedback.* For example, if they are entrenched in ideas such as insisting on having a white/UK social worker only, then the impact and potential success of the tool may be limited.

The starting point would be for individuals to accept that *everyone* (including social workers and other professionals) has personal prejudices, regardless of whether they were inherited through family values, acquired via peer and friendship groups, or attained by way of (social) media influences and so on, and, therefore, not to regard themselves as inadequate in any way. Acknowledging this at the outset aids in creating effective relationships and is a great way to break down barriers and help individuals to recognise that no one is perfect.

The **Ch-ch-ch-changes Model** is applied most effectively if the individual is given time and space to reflect on whatever incident or event is on their mind. Attempts by professionals to impose ideas onto the individual will only prove to undermine the process. Remember, just as for students, the starting place for people with lived experience might be resistance; however, an intense or acute encounter may catapult them straight to commitment (or vice versa).

'We can be "sheroes", "heroes" and "theyroes"'

I have always been intrigued by the notion of heroes and superheroes. As a child, I read and was fascinated by Marvel *and* DC *comic superheroes with their incredible strength and superpowers, their ability to thwart the baddie every time, save the city and strive for justice.* 'Superman', 'The Flash', 'Spiderman' *and* 'The Incredible Hulk' *were particular favourites of mine. Going into my early and mid-teens, it did not really occur to me that my 'favourite' superheroes were all white, able-bodied males (well, the professor of The Hulk's alter ego is before he turns green anyway!). Perhaps it was only when I reached mid-adolescence that I began to ponder who I was (from an ethnic perspective) and how these superheroes represented me. On reflection, Erikson's (1965, cited in Gibson and Gibson, 2016, p 68) 'Identity versus Role Confusion' stage and Phinney's (1993, cited in Walker, 2017, p 123) 'Ethnic Identity Development' model were catalysts for me to commence a journey of 'finding myself'. Upon coming into social work teaching, I have used my childhood experience of superhero worship and 'race' to support students to critically reflect on what is generally accepted as the status quo.*

Origins

Now for the interesting bit! Although there may well be similar exercises based on related or unrelated subjects, the idea of this exercise came to me while preparing to undertake a teaching session on the subject of 'black perspectives and white privilege' for first-year undergraduate students. Based on research from an article some colleagues and I had published that same year (Hollinrake et al, 2019), with one of the key summary points being that teaching of anti-racism on the programme should be conducted in 'safe spaces', I was eager to ensure that this was put into practice. Consequently, rather than approaching the session in the traditional 'lecture' format, I opted to use a workshop structure, with four or five chairs around tables. The next thing to do was to introduce the topic, and to strongly reinforce the message that 'we are all here to learn; no one is perfect, and it is okay to make mistakes – this is a space safe from criticism, harassment and persecution'. Once the basic, but very serious, ground rules were instilled, we were ready to begin.

This is a very uncomplicated, and yet highly effective, tool that practice educators can employ. The exercise can help to build relationships with students through the exploration of comic figures that have been brought to life on the big screen, more so if both the practice educator and student have a shared interest in the topic. Regardless, engaging in the exercise can be fun and enjoyable, allowing the student (and practice educator) to perhaps return to a forgotten aspect of their childhood, or to temporarily engross themselves in fantasy. All it requires is a pen/pencil and a little imagination...

Theory

The **Sheroes, Heroes and Theyroes** tool is largely based on theories of unconscious or cognitive bias and socialisation. It is said that as humans, biases play a major role in our lives as we look to solve problems, examine information, locate patterns and attempt to join the dots. Biases allow us to make quick decisions, take mental shortcuts and make educated guesses. When this happens, there is a danger of joining the dots in the wrong order or making ill-considered judgements (Smethurst, 2017; Zhou, 2020).

There is little doubt that western norms have reinforced the biased ways in which many of the individuals occupying this planet construct the way in which heroes and superheroes are perceived. Parsons (1951, cited in Cunningham and Cunningham, 2014, p 95) argues that human personality is not born, but made, and through the process of family socialisation our values and personalities are shaped. Linking this to 'joining the dots' in the minds of children, coupled with unconscious/cognitive bias, it is therefore apparent how our minds and preferences are formed from a very young age.

How does it work?

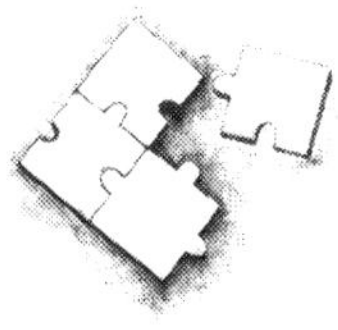

This **Sheroes, Heroes and Theyroes** tool can be undertaken during formal or informal supervision, for example, a shared car journey, in joint reflective discussions, or in small or large groups. It is also flexible in that it *does not have* to be about superheroes (acknowledging that not everyone is concerned with *Marvel* or *DC*!). In that way, comic-based superheroes can be exchanged for the students' own notion of a superhero or something as basic as describing the 'ideal girl, boy or person next door'. Essentially, what you are asking the student to do is describe the main skills, strengths, attributes, features and powers of their person of choice.

The exercise starts by giving the student five to ten minutes to think of a superhero (or ideal childhood neighbour) as described above. You should not rush them at this point and allow maximum thinking time. Once the time is up, ask them to bullet point the character's key features. Again, allow enough time for this. Once the time is up, ask the student to share their list. Bear in mind that if the student has selected a white person, they are unlikely to describe their ethnicity. If they have chosen a person of the global majorities, it is more likely they will include at least one ethnic characteristic. Once the student has shared the key characteristics of their person, you might ask questions such as the following.

- What inspired you to choose the person or character?
- Did you consciously select a white/black male/female/non-binary character; if so, why?
- If this was done subconsciously, why do you think this might be?
- Are you aware that when you described your person's characteristics, you included or excluded their ethnicity?
- What are your views on why there are so few black or global majorities superheroes?
- Can you see how white privilege might work in such instances?
- How do you think black people or people from the global majorities might feel about underrepresentation generally?
- On reflection, what are your thoughts and feelings now?

If the student selected a black or global majorities character, similar questions can be asked; however, the emphasis here might be more related to equality, diversity, inclusion and empowerment. For example, if they consciously selected a person of the global majorities, bullet point 4 and onwards would be helpful points to explore and assist the student to determine their thinking and positioning.

The key point of this exercise is to determine whether there are natural biases towards the sex and ethnicity of people or characters society reveres as heroic for one reason or another.

Invariably, and due to socialisation and unconscious bias, you will find that students will either select an 'obvious' white, male superhero, or perhaps the white female students will select or design a white, female character; however, the 'whiteness' of the character is seldom recognised or acknowledged – it is just taken for granted. It is at this point those discussions related to unconscious bias can be brought to life and how this can impact on students' perceptions of, and responses to, citizens.

I have undertaken this exercise with first-year social work students for three consecutive years now, and other than the black/'global majorities' students, the outcome has been pretty much the same. Ensuing discussions with students who describe being shocked with the outcome have resulted in students reflecting on their biases and white privilege and translating it into their academic essays and future social work practice more successfully.

How the tool can be utilised within social work practice

While social work students are required to meet and evidence professional standards (SWE, 2019) and frameworks (BASW, 2018), people with lived experience are not obligated to, nor are they compelled to reflect and consider their behaviour and actions following contact with other professionals. Having said that, those who may be in the early stages of anti-racist enlightenment (eg *resistance* or *exploration* – see **Ch-ch-ch-changes Model**) would no doubt find this exercise extremely helpful in connecting with their personal values and how it might translate if or when working with people from the global majorities.

For many individuals, it may be that the village/town/city they reside in is predominately white, and they may have never encountered people from the global majorities before. Their upbringing, socialisation and values could well be entrenched in white, westernised norms, and the allocation of a global majorities (student) social worker might take them out of their comfort zone. It is not unheard of for people with lived experience of health and social care to protest strongly at the prospect of having a key worker who does not match them racially. When 'choice' is denied in such circumstances, application of this simple exercise might prove to be a starting place for people, and a catalyst for change.

'It's a walk in the park...'

The following tool is one of the most challenging, yet intriguing, ones I have experienced during my social work and academic career, and highlights how unconscious bias, socialisation, whiteness and (internalised) racism manifests and festers without individuals realising. The tool was introduced to me and a small group of social work students by an external facilitator within a workshop related to 'Domestic Abuse and Diversity'. Although the facilitator would not claim to have invented the tool herself, its introduction during this workshop was simply astonishing and has forced me to critically reflect on my own position and views in relation to internalised racism and unconscious bias.

Origins

As explained above, I am unaware of the origins of this tool; however, not having this information does not undermine it in any way. As with the **Sheroes, Heroes and Theyroes** tool, inspiration can come from anywhere: the imagination, experiences, observations, through reading, watching the TV or through research. When individuals are inspired through a learning experience, it is quite remarkable how this can translate into theories, models, working tools and exercises.

What I love most about this particular tool is that it can be used with just about anyone, from early childhood (who might prefer to draw it) to older adults and everyone in between, in every walk of life, regardless of colour, social class, religious persuasion, sex or sexuality.

Theory

As with the **Sheroes, Heroes and Theyroes** tool, the theoretical underpinning of this tool is closely linked to unconscious, or *implicit bias*, stereotyping and socialisation, as well as encompassing cognitive dissonance. Implicit bias can be described as an unconscious association, belief or attitude towards any social group, and, consequently, individuals might ascribe specific qualities or characteristics to all members of the group accordingly. We regard the lazy practice of generalising social groups as *stereotyping*. It is value based, simplified and not evidenced informed.

The term *implicit bias* is attributed to Tony Greenwald and Mahzarin Banaji (1995) in the 1990s. Their theory of implicit social cognition was published later, in which they categorically state that the biases and social behaviour of individuals by and large correlate with unconscious, or implicit, judgements (Berghoef, 2019). The Implicit Association Test (IAT), developed from Greenwald's and Banaji's research, is now accepted as a tool to successfully measure individuals' implicit bias, or preferences, related to 'race', gender, weight and sexual orientation (Greenwald et al, 1998; Berghoef, 2019).

Festinger's (1957) theory of cognitive dissonance proposes that 'we don't know what we don't know', in which humans attempt to resolve 'psychological states of discomfort' when faced with contradicting thoughts and/or inconsistencies (Ogden and Biebers, 2010). It could be argued that it is only when our ignorance is challenged, and we move through step 2 of the process (the most difficult stage – true *dissonance*), that we might begin on a journey of self-awareness and personal development.

How does it work?

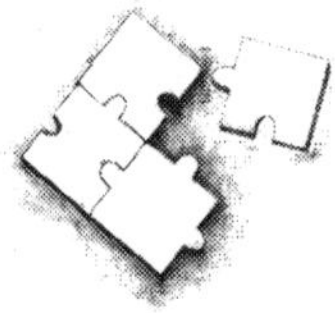

The **'It's a walk in the park...'** tool could be used effectively in supervision and/or as a critically reflective exercise by students. Again, it involves the use of the imagination.

Ask the student to close their eyes as they are about to go on a walk to the park. Ask them to imagine that they are at the front door of their home. It is a nice warm summer's day as they close the door and step outside.

1. Just as you are about to leave, the postie delivers some mail. ***Acknowledge them.***
2. You set off down the road and are immediately passed by a cyclist. ***Acknowledge them.***
3. A few minutes later, a couple, holding hands, pass you, going in the opposite direction. ***Acknowledge them.***
4. You arrive at the park and walk through the gates and pass a play area. Children are playing on the swings and in the sandpit, and parents sit close by, chatting, watching and playing with the children. ***Acknowledge them.***
5. After a while, you feel hot and thirsty so decide to get something to quench your thirst. You spot an ice-cream van nearby, where you purchase a drink and an ice-cream from the vendor. ***Acknowledge them.***
6. After a while, you decide to return home, passing the children and parents in the play area, but no one else as you make the same journey back to your front door and let yourself in.

Now, ask the student to repeat the journey aloud, but this time, ask them to *describe* the postie, the couple, the children, the parents and the ice-cream vendor.

Due to implicit bias, it is likely that a student will describe a white, male postie, a white, heterosexual couple, white boys, girls and 'mums' in the park, and a white, male ice-cream vendor. As Greenwald and Banaji's (1995) theory suggests, biases and judgements of most students completing the **'It's a walk in the park...'** tool are unlikely to consider other ethnic groups, disabilities or sexuality, and will more often place adults into gendered roles (ie the postie and ice-cream vendor are more likely to be 'male' and the parents with the children 'female'). The beauty of this tool is that it can used as an intersectional tool (how ethnicity, sex, disability and sexuality overlap and connect with one another), or simply to determine biases related to 'race', gender, disability and sexuality.

I had not undertaken nor seen this exercise previously. Although the facilitator shared it as a student experience, I also chose to join in. By the end of it, I was shocked at my own unconscious and implicit bias, as well as remnants of internalised racism I thought I had resolved many years previously.

I discovered that I too had fallen into the 'trap' (if that is the right word – certainly not the intention) of seeing the people on my journey as white, able-bodied, heterosexual, socially gendered males and females. This immediately sparked thoughts around my own cognitive dissonance (Festinger, 1957; see ***Ch-ch-ch-changes Model*** *above). I found myself questioning my own values, status and position in relation to human rights and social justice.*

It might be assumed by some that people from the global majorities, including myself, are more likely to 'see' people like ourselves on this simple journey; however, here at least is some evidence that someone who is committed to anti-racism, who teaches black history, anti-racism, black perspectives and whiteness, who was raised in a black family, in a reasonably diverse part of a town, can also think like the majority of the UK population, so how much more so for white students living in non-diverse towns, cities and villages? The beauty of such a revelation for me, however, is not to beat ourselves up over our limitations, but to accept them, critically reflect, learn and grow.

How the tool can be utilised within social work practice

I guess the first question is do people with lived experience need to know about their cognitive, unconscious and implicit biases? Whether or not we believe the answer is a simple 'yes' or 'no', this is a straightforward tool that can be carried out with limited fuss and absolutely no judgement.

As with the previous tools, logically, only those individuals wanting to go on a journey of self-discovery are likely to gain any real benefit from it; however, for those that do, it is a matter of what they do with it once their biases are revealed.

It is interesting to note that official figures show that the number of black social workers in England increased between September 2017 and September 2020 (to 12.3 per cent), with the figure for Asian social workers at 5.6 per cent (Department for Education, 2021). This clearly suggests that the chances of individuals working with a social worker from the global majorities at some stage is even more possible than in previous years. The foundations of effective, anti-oppressive, person-centred, relationship-based and solution-focused practice can only realistically be developed and applied if individuals (and social workers) acknowledge their biases and look to work from positions of respect and equality.

Three key points

1. Just as it is said that 'safeguarding is everyone's responsibility', then it could be argued that the fight for a fair and equal society is too. The difference here is that we are talking about social work education and practice; therefore, practice educators have a major responsibility in that regard. As defined by the International Federation of Social Workers (IFSW, 2014), '*principles of social justice, human rights, collective responsibility and respect for diversities are central to social work*' – and are things we should be fighting *for* collectively and not ignoring due to ignorance, privilege, fear or any other reason. As a well-known saying goes, '*if you are not part of the solution, you are part of the problem*'.

2. When it comes to the subject of anti-racism, it would be presumptuous and dangerous to place anyone in the position of 'expert', be this in relation to lived experience, education or a combination of the two. As practice educators, it is imperative that honest and open conversations take place with students from the outset. If you set yourself up as 'the expert', students may well rely on your specialist knowledge as opposed to undertaking their own research. Not taking role of expert from the outset can help to reduce the power element and create a more conducive and respectful environment.

3. The topics of 'race' and racism are extremely emotive subjects. Due to personal trauma, experiences, guilt, fragility and resistance, there may well be difficult and emotional times when discussing the topic and undertaking the exercises. What needs to be borne in mind is that it is more important to have the conversation than to pretend that racism doesn't exist, 'doesn't happen here' or only happens in certain places/communities. The impact of historical practices, globalisation, extremism and civil and regionalised war results in individuals, families and whole communities migrating to Europe and the UK in the hope of better living. It is surely better to have some knowledge of best working practices (in this case anti-racist) than to start on the back foot as it were.

I would like to acknowledge and thank Tonia Wilson for her inspiration, contribution and permission to share the final tool within this chapter.

References

Berghoef, K (2019) Implicit Bias: What It Means and How It Affects Behavior. [online] Available at: www.thoughtco.com/understanding-implicit-bias-4165634 (accessed 20 February 2022).

British Association of Social Workers (BASW) (2018) Professional Capabilities Framework. [online] Available at: www.basw.co.uk/social-work-training/professional-capabilities-framework-pcf (accessed 20 February 2022).

Cunningham, J and Cunningham, S (2014) *Sociology & Social Work*. 2nd ed. London: Sage/Learning Matters.

Department for Education (2021) Social Workers for Children and Families. [online] Available at: www.ethnicity-facts-figures.service.gov.uk/workforce-and-business/workforce-diversity/social-workers-for-children-and-families/latest (accessed 20 February 2022).

Festinger, L (1957) *A Theory of Cognitive Dissonance.* Stanford, CA: Stanford University Press.

Gibson, A and Gibson, N (2016) *Human Growth, Behaviour and Development*. London: Sage.

Greenwald, A G and Banaji, M R (1995) Implicit Social Cognition: Attitudes Self-Esteem, and Stereotypes. *Psychological Review*, 102(1): 4–27.

Greenwald, A G, McGhee, D and Schwartz, J L K (1998) Measuring Individual Differences in Implicit Cognition: The Implicit Association Test. *Journal of Personality and Social Psychology*, 74(6): 1464–80.

Hollinrake, S, Hunt, G, Dix, H and Wagner, A (2019) Do We Practice (or Teach) What We Preach? Developing a More Inclusive Learning Environment to Better Prepare Social Work Students for Practice Through Improving the Exploration of Their Different Ethnicities within Teaching, Learning and Assessment Opportunities. *Social Work Education (International Journal)*, 38(5): 582–603.

International Federation of Social Workers (IFSW) (2014) Global Definition of Social Work. [online] Available at: www.ifsw.org/what-is-social-work/global-definition-of-social-work (accessed 20 February 2022).

Kendi, I X (2020) The Difference Between 'Not Racist' and Antiracist. [online] Available at: www.ted.com/talks/ibram_x_kendi_the_difference_between_being_not_racist_and_antiracist (accessed 20 February 2022).

Kübler-Ross, E (1969) *On Death and Dying: What the Dying Have to Teach Doctors, Nurses, Clergy, and Their Own Families*. New York: Scribner.

Ogden, S K and Biebers, A D (2010) *Psychology of Denial*. New York: Nova Science.

Scott, C D and Jaffe, D T (1988) Survive and Thrive in Times of Change. *Training and Development Journal*, 42(4): 25–7.

Smethurst, C (2017) Class, Inequality, and Social Work: 'We're All In This Together?' In Bhatti-Sinclair, K and Smethurst, C (eds) *Diversity, Difference and Dilemmas* (pp 49–61). London: Open University Press.

Social Work England (SWE) (2019) Professional Standards. [online] Available at: www.socialworkengland.org.uk/standards/professional-standards (accessed 20 February 2022).

Stroebe, M and Schut, H (2010) The Dual Process Model of Coping with Bereavement: A Decade On. *OMEGA – Journal of Death and Dying*, 61(4): 273–89.

The British Psychological Society (2020) Education is the Most Powerful Weapon Which You Can Use to Change the World. *Black History Month* blog. [online] Available at: www.bps.org.uk/blogs/black-history-month/education-most-powerful-weapon (accessed 20 February 2022).

Thompson, N and British Association of Social Workers (2021) *Anti-discriminatory Practice: Equality, Diversity and Social Justice*. 7th ed. London: Red Globe Press.

Walker, J (2017) *Social Work and Human Development*. London: Sage/ Learning Matters.

Zhou Q and 2020 IEEE International Professional Communication Conference, ProComm 2020 (2020) Cognitive Biases in Technical Communication. *IEEE International Professional Communication Conference*, July 2020, pp 39–46. doi:10.1109/ProComm48883.2020.00012.

Can you see me?

Lanai Collis-Phillips

Can you see me as I lie under my sheets, the
overwhelming fear surrounding me, but the next
day I am in school promising everything is okay

Can you see me when I am a missing child as my
groomers have taken me away or is it easier for you
to believe I am just another runaway

Can you see me for me when the media turns my
passion into aggression, the relentless ignorant
comments and questions on my hair, my culture
just perpetuating our oppression

Can you see me when I get stopped and searched
9.7 times more than my white counterpart

Can you see me before I have to die at the hands
of a knife or will I be just another statistic in the chart?

Chapter 4

The creative use of timelines: A trauma-sensitive approach for developing students' critical analysis and reflexivity

Caroline Aldridge

Introduction

Social workers help people make sense of their life journeys and they use sequencing, such as chronologies or trajectories, in their day-to-day practice. Many of the people who need social work assessments or interventions will have trauma histories. Therefore, a vital element of social worker training is enabling students to work in trauma-sensitive ways. This chapter will offer ideas to practice educators about using timelines to assist social work students in developing their direct work skills, critical analysis, application of theory, planning, reflexivity, empathy, understanding of self, and use of digital technology.

The experiential use of timelines can support students to develop insight into their histories, which may include previous trauma, and how this might impact on their practice. Practice educators have a key role in facilitating students to develop reflexivity through modelling trauma-sensitive practice. The chapter will begin by considering what is meant by trauma-sensitive practice education and offers suggestions for activities to use in supervision sessions within emotionally safe boundaries.

Trauma-sensitive practice education

Trauma is defined as *'an exposure to an extraordinary experience that presents a physical or psychological threat to oneself or others and generates a reaction of helplessness and fear'* (Levenson, 2017, p 105). Social workers need to *'modulate their responses to trauma'* so they can be empathic while maintaining their own equilibrium (Greer, 2016, p 49). In essence, a trauma-sensitive social worker recognises the prevalence of trauma and how this might impact on people's social, psychological, emotional, and cognitive development.

Trauma sensitivity recognises the coping strategies people might employ and embraces relationship- and strengths-based approaches. It is widely recognised that health and social care professions attract people who might have lived experiences or trauma histories. Thus, trauma might be situated within the person requiring services, the student, or practitioner. Consequently, social workers will be directly affected (Harms, 2015).

Before undertaking any piece of creative work that could be triggering, it is important to identify some 'emotional brakes' and to think about when and how they will be applied. It is fundamental that the student is allowed to control what and how they share. Being explicit about this enables practice educators to model a key direct work skill. In a short YouTube video, psychotherapist Babette Rothschild (2009) uses a wonderful analogy of shaking up a cola bottle to explain this. She posits that when working with trauma we should gently open the lid to release some pressure but be ready to firmly close it again before things get messy. This concept is applicable to social workers' practice but also to educators. Taking the analogy further, if we leave the lid untouched there is a risk that at any point something could cause it to come off. Nevertheless, it is not the practice educator's role to delve into a student's trauma and this could be harmful (Rothschild, 2010), although it is important to maintain a trauma-sensitive approach.

Below is a framework to emotionally contain and structure a creative practice session.

Before Think about your student and what they might find enjoyable or difficult. Choose your activity carefully and consider what preparations are needed. Identify an emotionally neutral back-up activity to use if you need to apply the brakes.
At the beginning Be explicit about your aims and purpose. Agree some boundaries with the student (for example, clarifying that they can choose what to share or stop if they wish). Give a trigger warning and agree with the student how they want to be supported if they do become dysregulated.

During Be attentive and affirming. Attune to the student and take notice of non-verbal clues. Use open questions such as, 'tell me more about...'
At the end Close the activity down and return to something positive. Reflect on the activity.

The social work student journey can be emotionally demanding. Previously emotionally regulated students might find themselves struggling with unresolved trauma or loss. People find strategies for managing trauma and preventing it from spilling out in an uncontrolled way, but when we start exploring people's histories or emotions we can inadvertently trigger a response. Even the simplest activity can provoke an unexpected reaction. Students commonly express surprise at how emotional they feel when creating a timeline.

> I became very anxious when recalling some events and started to get thoughts in my head, particularly when acknowledging my PTSD diagnosis. I had to take some time away and remember how far I have come since then.

Being trauma-sensitive requires proceeding at the student's pace. The need for time to think, reflect, take breaks and process is a theme in students' reflections.

> I have started and stopped this activity several times as there are many events in my life I don't want exposed...

> I became absorbed in the activity... and spent more than the allotted time...

For some students or practice educators, their trauma might reflect an intersection of multiple traumas or oppressions, such as those relating to disability, gender, race, or religion. Theories of assimilation assume that people from global majority backgrounds should adapt to white British society (Graham, 2007). Tyler (2020) graphically explains the insidiousness of racism, based on the UK's colonial history that is embedded in our society. It is omnipresent yet unrecognised and rooted in abuses of power. Tyler asserts that racism is experienced as a '*highly sophisticated form of violence*' (2020, p 15) that leaves invisible scars. So, students from global majority backgrounds are likely to have an additional layer of trauma that can impact their confidence and sense of self.

Looking backwards

The inspiration for the use of timelines comes from the tools I have used in trauma-informed therapeutic work with children and families. Over time, a psychodynamic theoretical base was overlaid with elements relating to neuroscience and developmental trauma. As I moved into practice education, I adapted the tools to support students.

In social work we use timelines and chronologies to look back and compile the history of people's lives or a situation. The identification of significant events, patterns, or triggers can support critical analysis. Sorting information and putting it in chronological order helps to make sense of things.

Critical analysis of chronologies cards

Ask the student to reflect on a chronology they have undertaken and consider what they noticed in the recordings they drew the information from. A way of making this more engaging is to create question cards.

Here are some question examples.

How were the documents you looked at written? Did they differ in terms of tone and format for different audiences?	Did you come across jargon or acronyms? Did you understand all the terms used?

What aspects of the recordings were helpful? Why?	Did you spot documents that seemed excellent? What was it about them that you liked?
What information did you find about the person's culture, race, religion or ethnicity?	How easy or difficult was it to find the information you needed? Why?
How culturally sensitive were the documents you looked at?	How did the culture of the child, family or community inform assessments and interventions?
Imagine the documents were written about your life – how would you feel?	Did you identify any worrying patterns or trigger points?
How easy would the child or adult being written about find reading these documents? Why?	How reliable was the information you drew on? What criteria did you use to weigh information?
Why did you select the entries for the chronology? How easy or difficult was it to choose? Or to summarise?	Was any of the language used judgemental and value-laden (such as 'mum', 'dad', 'difficult family', 'failed', 'toxic')?
Did you notice assumptions, gaps or unsubstantiated 'facts'?	Did you see any application of theory in the documents you looked at?
How did the practice documented align with approaches and frameworks used in the practice setting?	What theories could you use to explain the documents you viewed or the chronology you created?

Lifelines and timelines

Lifelines, used therapeutically (with a small 't'), are features of many interventions used with adults and children. Theoretical underpinning can be found in texts relating to lifestory work, psychotherapy, and mental health. The aims are broadly the same: to identify significant events to prompt therapeutic conversations. Lifelines can help people make sense of their life experiences by putting events into chronological order.

In its simplest form, these can be drawn on a piece of paper (Figure 4.1) and key positive and negative events noted down on a line. Therefore, this can be a spontaneous activity to use whenever there is a need to understand a sequence of past events.

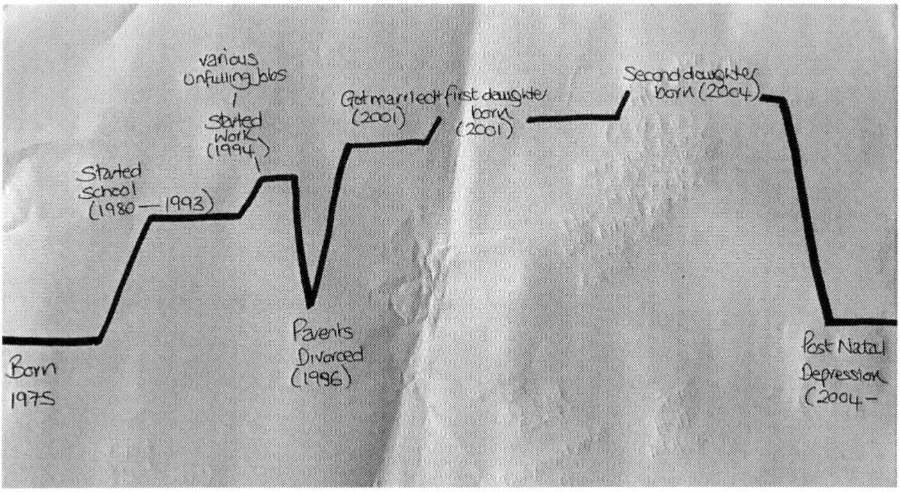

Figure 4.1 Lifelines

However, even the most basic timeline can be highly triggering. Those like the example above starkly illustrate the extremes of emotion attached to events.

> …despite how simple and brief it was… it reminded me that, like lots of people, I have had a hard life in many ways and that I am who I am, good and bad, as a result of this…

Nevertheless, being more creative can enable people to express themselves more easily or feel soothed by a multi-sensory approach. For example, a student created a timeline in her garden using a photograph of some images and text placed on the ground (Figure 4.2). She said:

> Initially I was worried [about my creative abilities] but then I started to formulate ideas, starting from what I enjoy (gardening) and then I started to relax and enjoy it. It made me forget about other things and got me thinking creatively.

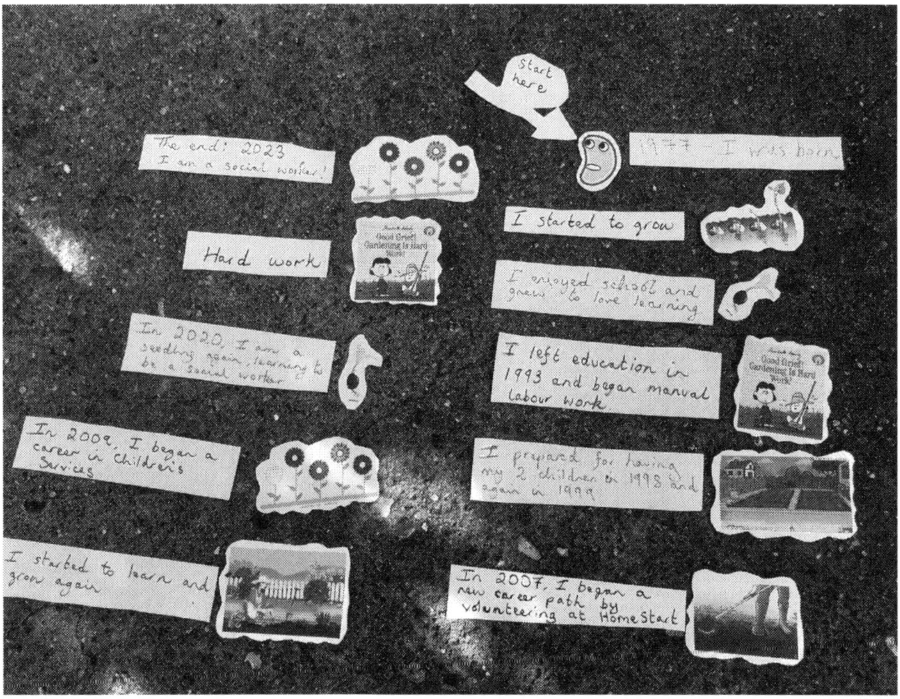

Figure 4.2 Timeline with photographs

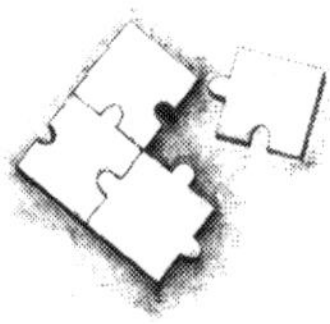

There are infinite variations of lifelines and plenty of scope to be creative and adapt the activity according to age, interests and purpose.

Lifelines might be presented as maps, graphs, journeys or flow-charts. With minimal preparation and resources, the activity can be elevated into a richer learning experience through the use of scale, colour and images.

It is helpful for students to make explicit links to practice. Encourage them to think about different groups of individuals and social work roles and then consider how they might use timelines or lifelines. Discuss what they might need in their emotional or physical 'tool box'.

There is added value in practising an activity with a practice educator. This enables the student to observe how an experienced practitioner uses the tools and how they navigate the feelings evoked by the activity. However, when creating a timeline with their practice educator, the student might feel under pressure to disclose, or feel exposed if they have emotional reactions. Given the power dynamics in the practice educator and student relationship, it might feel less oppressive to allow the student to complete their timeline privately and bring it to the session. However the timeline is created, a trauma-sensitive practice educator needs to be alert to signs of discomfort or dysregulation and offer reassurance or redirect to a calming activity.

Wallpaper journey

You will need a length of wallpaper (or some sheets of paper joined together) and coloured pens. The activity can be enhanced through the use of photographs, images, stickers, or anything that could be used in a multi-media collage.

You might want to ask your student to prepare by bringing some materials they want to use. Decide on a format – will this be a track, road or river? Choose a theme or purpose such as unpicking an aspect of the student's life to help them understand their experiences. Be trauma-sensitive and remember this is not therapy. Allow the student to choose what they disclose.

A student who created a ladder (Figure 4.3) with dates and drawn symbols said:

> It felt important to me to only publish the year and image to a wider audience. This keeps a level of privacy and ownership of life events.

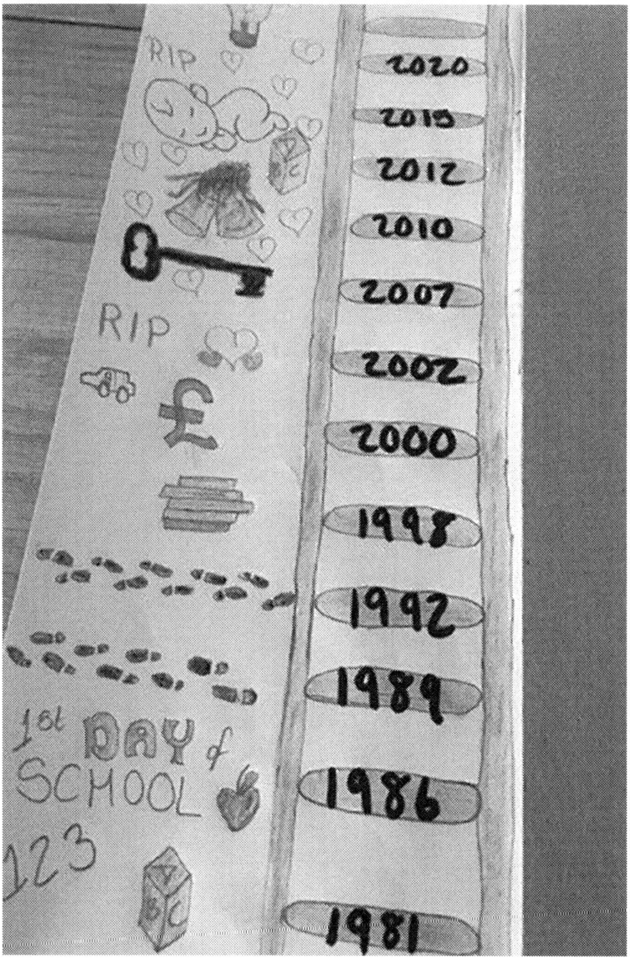

Figure 4.3 Ladder

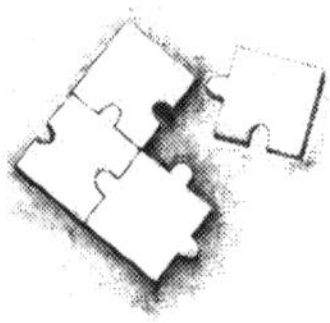

Be aware that the student might be surprised by what surfaces (in welcome or unwelcome ways). Even selecting what to leave in or out can be triggering.

> I felt quite worried about what kind of memories would be provoked during the activity and also wanted to consider how much I was ready or willing to share...

A relatively neutral starting point might be the student's academic journey. Consider where you will ask your student to begin their lifeline. It is usually less emotive to start in the present. If reflecting on the past triggers difficult feelings, these need acknowledging and containing by grounding in the present or looking forward to something hopeful.

Creating a lifeline can be done privately or collaboratively. The key thing is the conversations it generates. We need to really listen carefully with all our senses and use this as a starting point for exploration. Extend the learning from the activity by modelling curiosity and asking questions such as the following.

- Did anything surprise you?
- Can you identify any antecedents?
- Reflecting on the activity, can you identify when other people positively or negatively impacted on the direction of your journey?
- How did you feel undertaking the activity? How might your feelings influence the likelihood of using this tool? Or the way you might use it?
- How did the relationship with the practice educator (who holds power) influence what you disclosed or kept private?
- How does this activity fit with your culture?
- What was included? Or left out? Why might that be?

- Were you able to put things in a coherent order or are events confused?
- Can you make links to the wider context (such as attitudes and socio-political context)?
- What have you learnt that will influence your practice?
- What theories could explain any of the above?

The purpose of undertaking a lifeline activity is learning. Students need to reflect on activities and identify when and how they might use timelines with the people who they work with.

> This exercise reinforced how a person with lived experience may feel sharing their life journey and how some things you don't want to revisit and can awake inner feelings and memories.

> It made me consider the impact that lifestory work can have on a child... it is definitely a powerful tool and something I will need to think about in future.

> If I was doing this with someone else, I would probably start with now and perhaps work backwards, or I might pick out significant events and fill in the gaps. I don't know if there is a right or wrong way to approach this...

Looking forwards

Students will use trajectories in their practice because planning is important to prevent drift. Clear plans can create certainty in uncertain situations. For example, social workers might not be able to answer a question such as whether a child will return home, but they can indicate when the decision will be made and mark out points of certainty, such as visits, in the interim. Signs of Safety® (an approach used in many local authorities and settings) uses trajectories as a transparent way of clarifying what steps families need to make in order for goals to be achieved. When parents and carers are provided with a '*clear, time-tabled trajectory*' that details what needs to happen with stages, this '*makes the expectations more concrete*' and provides hope (Turnell, 2013, p 13).

Having clear plans and creating some certainty in pressurised or fluid situations is emotionally containing. This is equally applicable to students as to those who use services. Social work students are often juggling work, study and home life. Many have caring responsibilities or have lived experiences (which has the potential to enhance their insight and empathy but also means that they might find practice placements challenging).

Time management and organisational skills are key in developing professional resilience; breaking things down into small steps is effective because people feel a sense of control (Grant and Kinman, 2014).

Planning

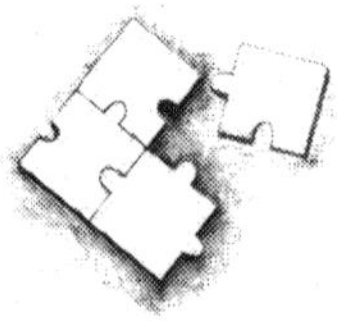

Supporting students to plan can be an opportunity to be creative. For example, creating a week-by-week map, on a single sheet with all the placement milestones and deadlines, can help both practice educator and student see how to spread the workload and monitor progress.

Anyone might benefit from visual plans or 'easy read' versions that easily map out deadlines. Engaging people with plans and creating a sense of ownership can be reinforced by being creative and co-creating the timeline. While any writing, cutting, sticking, drawing or decorating takes place, the plans can be agreed and reinforced through conversation.

There is no limit to the creativity that can be employed using supplies from the stationery cupboard: rockets with countdowns; mountain pathways; posters; calendars; cards on a string; and numbered envelopes. There are many templates for planners available online. Trajectories can be drawn on the beach, written on bunting or labels tied to trees, or even stuck to the risers of stairs! If a plan is created in an ephemeral way, then you need to take photographs as a record or aide-mémoire.

Adapting to virtual learning

Since Covid-19, social workers and students have needed to adapt and find virtual ways of working and studying (see Chapter 2). Some students might be underconfident in their use of digital technology and others might be highly skilled. Therefore, the shift to remote working has provided an opportunity to develop digital skills and creates the potential for educators to learn with and from their students.

Timelines can be easily adapted to virtual approaches. The practice educator has a role in helping students to think through possible pitfalls and ensure they are practising within professional and organisational boundaries. This might be a good opportunity to help the student explore issues of confidentiality, data protection and record keeping.

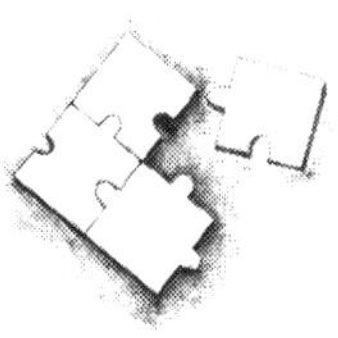

In practice-education sessions, it might be helpful to explore with students how they might use timelines for planning in their practice. Encourage them to evaluate their own organisational and planning skills. If they require support with this, consider where that might come from, then make links to practice. Ask the student to consider how easy or difficult a person with lived experience or carer might find planning. It's really important here to consider the student's ability to set and work with trajectories and their expectations of others.

Creating a timeline using digital tools

Figure 4.4 is a timeline created using a Word document.

Figure 4.4 Timeline using words

A PowerPoint with images, set to music and with automated slide change, can tell a powerful story. PowerPoint's 'slide-sorter' function makes it easy to add in slides and get the chronological order correct. This method enables the 'I am not creative' students to create something evocative through the use of text and images.

> I have never used PowerPoint with music, animations and transitions... Once I had completed the task, I had a sense of pride in what I had achieved.

Timelines can be easily created using tablets or phones. For example, photos in a mashup or album can be sorted into order and videos or podcasts are easily edited. There are a range of tools on devices that students will have access to, where images, documents and videos can be embedded.

Creating a timeline or trajectory using home resources

Share with the student some information about timelines and trajectories before asking for one to be created at home. The document or photograph of their artefact can then be shared with you or, if working with a group of students, on a closed group using Padlet®, which is a free online pinboard. Students can use any means they wish, including going outside, and can choose what aspect, ie looking forward or back, to explore. Following this activity, students could be asked to complete a written reflective evaluation to add another dimension to their learning.

In my experience, students demonstrate their resourcefulness and imagination when undertaking this activity. From toys laid out on the floor, through to a washing line with key points pegged out, their individual approaches and stories were captured beautifully. Students have conveyed aspects of their heritage and culture with several students sharing that they were born in or had lived in different countries.

Some students looked at their journey into social work and their aspirations. For example, a re-purposed Monopoly board (Figure 4.5) or map of islands (Figure 4.6).

Figure 4.5 Monopoly board

Many board games follow trajectories or convey a passage of time. Therefore, they are easily to convert to timelines. The game 'Snakes and Ladders' is particularly relevant with its ups and downs. Like most people's lives there are times of rapid progress and then tumbles following significant life events. In practice education sessions, students could be encouraged to create a lifeline board game. They could go deeper with this activity by making links to theories.

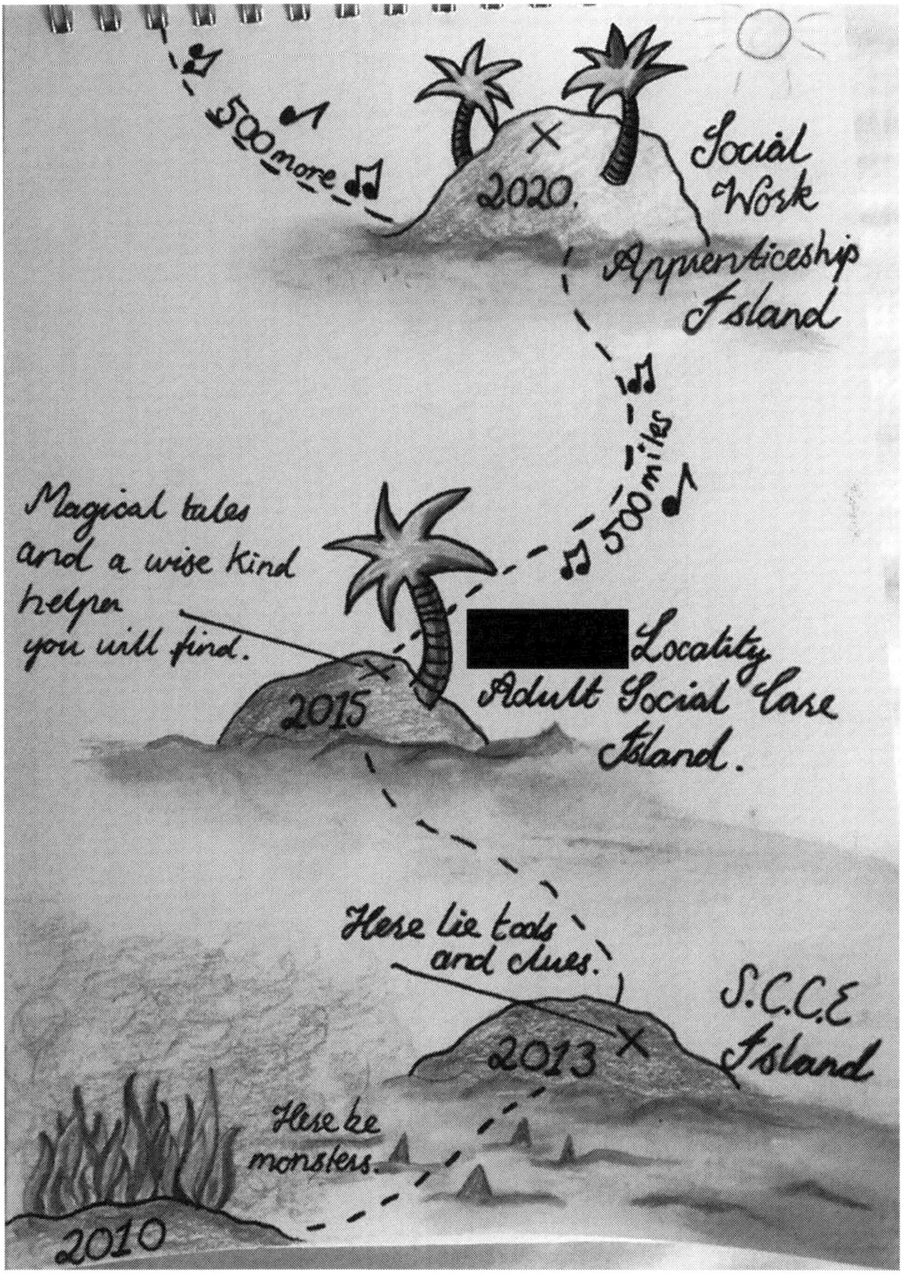

Figure 4.6 Map of islands

Some students attempted the activity using unfamiliar materials, whereas others chose to use methods they would find soothing because of the sensory element. One student created a stitched account of their early years. (Figure 4.7). In their reflections they realised how the different needlework techniques used mirrored how life was at that time:

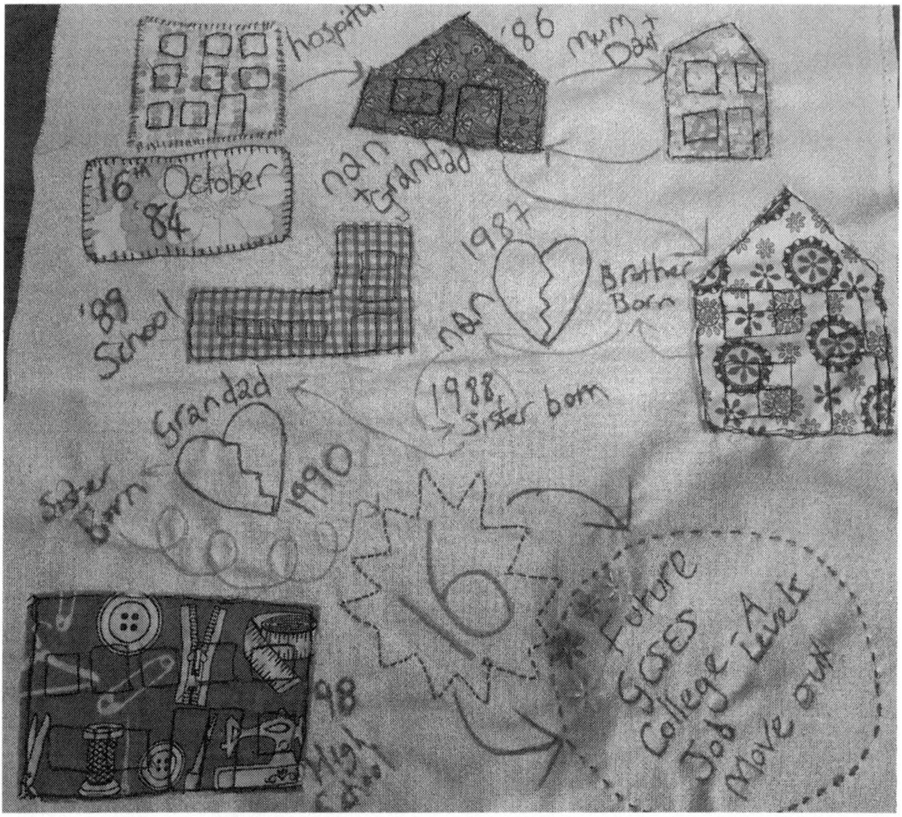

Figure 4.7 Stitched journey

> I find sewing very calming, so it was relaxing and absorbing... I felt very free to concentrate on what I was doing and how it made me feel: reflective, sad at times and happy at other points.

Maximising the learning from creating timelines

It is worth returning to any timelines created and reviewing or adding to them at least once. If students have created a timeline to bring to a supervision session, it is important that you look carefully and use it as a foundation for discussion or further development. It could form the basis for reflective writing or for assisting a student in exploring something they are struggling with.

Some examples of timelines used with students include the following.

- Think through plans for a child moving between foster placements and link to theory, their own experiences, and values.
- Reflect on one child's experience within a family.
- Unpick events that led to an older person requiring care and link to life-span theories.
- Identify cultural traditions and unpick how culture is experienced by a student.

One area that the creative use of timelines can help students to develop is empathy because they 'feel' what being asked about one's life is like. For example:

> Until I created my own timeline, I really had not thought about how uncomfortable it can be to reflect on significant events. Even the good times stir up emotions. We do this with service users all the time.

> The questions we ask in assessments are like the timeline. What has happened in your life? Where do you want to go? I understand more how exposing, or even frightening, this feels...

Summary

Timelines are a versatile tool that can be used to support students' learning in a wide variety of ways. Digital technologies can be utilised to adapt to virtual practice education and to support students in developing direct work skills.

Three key points

1. Trauma-sensitive practice education provides emotional safety and models good practice. Whether they are working with a student to reflect on experiences, process their emotions and develop reflexivity, or supporting them to plan effectively, practice educators are in a unique position to embrace the creative use of timelines and use these for deep learning and critical analysis.

2. Timelines are a versatile tool that can be used to support students' learning in a wide variety of ways. They can be used as a critical reflection tool, to develop therapeutic direct work skills or for planning.

3. Digital technologies can be utilised to adapt to virtual practice education and to support students in developing direct work skills.

Acknowledgement: The quotes and the images are from a cohort of first-year social work apprentices from Norfolk who kindly agreed to share the timelines they created and their reflective evaluations.

References

Graham, M (2007) *Black Issues in Social Work and Social Care*. Bristol: The Policy Press.

Grant, L and Kinman, G (2014) *Developing Resilience in Social Work Practice.* Basingstoke: Palgrave.

Greer, J (2016) *Resilience and Personal Effectiveness for Social Workers*. London: Sage.

Harms, L (2015) *Understanding Trauma and Resilience*. Basingstoke: Palgrave.

Levenson, J (2017) Trauma-Informed Social Work Practice. *Social Work*, 62(2): 105–13.

Rothschild, B (2009) Safe Trauma Recovery. [online] Available at: www.youtube.com/watch?v=LhuzpUlaX_k (accessed 20 February 2022).

Rothschild, B (2010) *8 Keys to Safe Trauma Recovery: Take Charge Strategies to Empower Your Healing.* London: W. W. Norton.

Turnell, A (2013) *Signs of Safety®: Safety Planning Workbook.* East Perth, WA: Resolutions Consultancy Pty Ltd.

Tyler, I (2020) *Stigma: The Machinery of Inequality.* London: Zed Books Ltd.

Swimming

Amanda Hodgkinson

The beach is a steep, shingle bank
so that running barefoot
into the sea at full pelt
– and how else to do it?
turns you to a bent knee,
hands-splayed silhouette.
Already your adult shape
is losing ground, heels sink,
letting go, you trust
the waters hold you,
your pulse rising
to the rhythm of waves

You will know, my love
the depths and shallows
the losing and the gaining heart
how sunlight glints on seawater
floating far from shore
where it dazzles like salt-starred
daisies in the breeze.
The beach is a steep tilt
leading to the sea.
I suggest you run down it,
barefoot at full pelt.

Chapter 5

Purpose, position, power and rights

Heidi Dix and Aisha Howells

Introduction

Power is potentially the most important theoretical concept in social work practice and embedded within the fabric of the profession's values and ethics. However, given its significance and how it is generally understood, there is no agreed definition. Instead, power is multidimensional and complex; put simply, it involves an ability to '*get things done*' (Thompson, 2018, p 60). Thinking about this in its broadest sense, the work of social workers is fundamentally about the use of various kinds of power, where we are positioned and how power influences and shapes practice and judgements. For example, it can be seen in how practitioners arrive at an assessment outcome and what recommendations and/or resource allocations follow. In terms of thinking about power between a student and practice educator, it plays an integral part within this relationship.

In your learning with the student, there are many different theories, models and frameworks of power that you may draw upon. You may be more familiar with power being seen as a negative and oppressive force, and often linked to discrimination, particularly given the interplay of the power inequalities in the learning relationship between a practice educator and a student. However, the purpose of this chapter is to provide practical remedies to engage with power constructively. Using these tools will help you consider how power needs to be interacted with and understood as it is key to the work you do as practice educators, students and practitioners. The tools will support you to deepen your knowledge, broaden your skills and enhance your confidence around power. They are resources that can be used to facilitate an honest and transparent approach to the way in which power is used.

Purpose, Position and Power tool

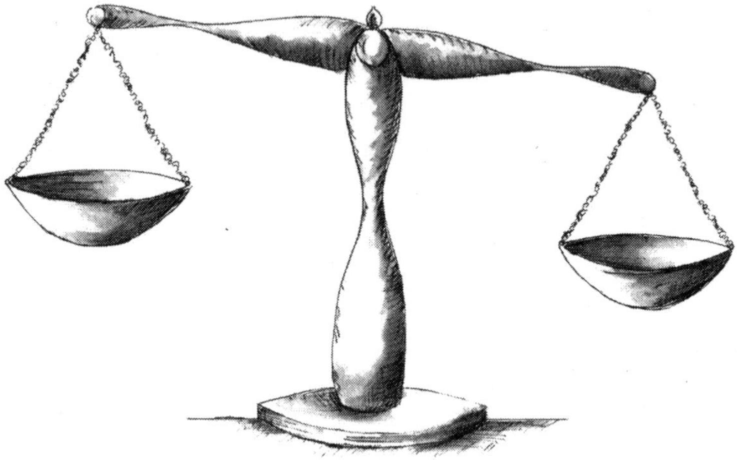

The need for practitioners to have knowledge of 'self' is well established within social work and activities to support self-awareness are threaded throughout prequalifying social work courses. However, understanding self is a lifelong endeavour and this **Purpose, Position and Power** tool has been designed to be undertaken by practice educators during any stage of their career to enable a greater understanding of the personal internal and external motivational factors for choosing to work with students in a practice educator role. This awareness is necessary as the views we hold about power and authority can influence the thoughts and feelings we have about students, which can have a direct impact on the provision of an effective anti-racist, anti-oppressive and anti-discriminatory learning environment. Some of the reflective activities within this tool can be adapted for use with students either individually or in groups to discuss motivation and introduce ideas of power within social work practice.

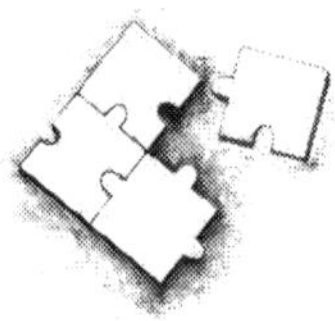

The **Purpose, Position and Power** tool is split into three reflective activities and ideally these are completed sequentially by the practice educator, although they can be standalone tasks. The first two reflective tasks can also be used as an exercise with students and suggestions have been provided as to how these can be adapted. The third exercise has been designed as a reflective activity for practice educators. However, you may have your own ideas as to how this can be modified for use alongside a student.

I was born with a disability and as a white working-class woman I was acutely aware of the power professionals held. During my education as a social work student, I observed social workers and practice educators using and misusing their personal and professional power with citizens and have had an interest in power and how it is used since. I have been privileged to work alongside colleagues who have used their professional power skilfully to make a positive difference and I have also witnessed occasions when this professional power has not been used to good effect. Recently, I have been involved in research, and during focus groups, students commented that they noticed and valued practice educators who took a genuine interest in their individual needs. This resonated with me and what these students were describing was practice educators using their power effectively to build relationships as the foundation for an effective learning environment.

Part 1: Purpose

Reflective activity for a practice educator part 1: Purpose

- ❖ What motivated you to become a practice educator?
- ❖ Make a list of at least five reasons why you decided to become a practice educator.
- ❖ Have any of these reasons changed over time? Why? Why not?
- ❖ What keeps you motivated as a practice educator?

Reflective activity for a practice educator to use with a student part 1: Purpose

Practice educators can begin this activity by asking students to list the reasons they decided to undertake their social work training. This is a question I ask early in the practice learning opportunity, and sometimes at the pre-placement meeting, as it often provides a valuable insight into the desires and motivations of students. Knowing this helps me to tailor the learning opportunities that can be made available to the student. This question also begins to explore concepts of power, which can be revisited during supervision sessions using the reflective activities within this tool. It is interesting to revisit the question at the end of the practice learning opportunity to see if the student has changed their thoughts in any way.

Part 2: Position

The views we have of power and authority could determine how comfortable we are with some aspects of the practice educator role than others. French and Raven (1959) identified five ways in which power exists, one of which is legitimate power where an individual holds power related to their position, title or role. As social work is a regulated profession with statutory duties, legitimate power is inherent within this identity, and it is necessary to consider how it is utilised in a non-oppressive way to work collaboratively with individuals. In addition, it could be suggested that social workers also hold other forms of power described by French and Raven such as expert power, since they have the knowledge, skills and values that inform social work practice. Practice educators also hold legitimate power as well as the expert power intrinsic to the role; both of these need to be understood and used to good effect.

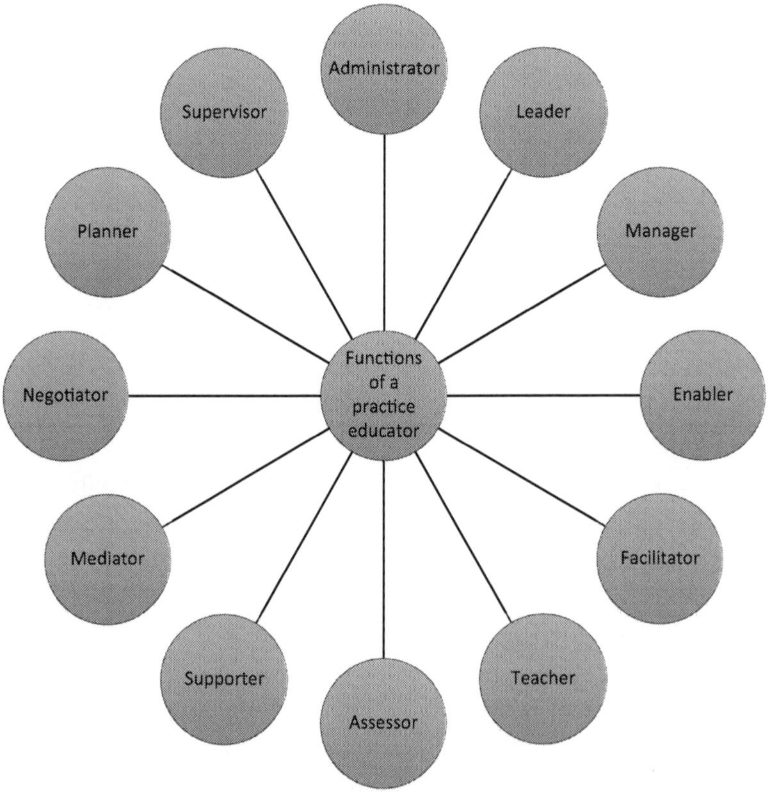

Figure 5.1 Functions of a practice educator

Reflective activity to be undertaken by a practice educator part 2: Position

I have adapted Field et al's (2014) description of the various functions contained within the practice education role, all of which contain different aspects of power (see Figure 5.1).

Look at the different functions involved in the practice education role. You may wish to add more to the list. Identify the aspects you feel more comfortable with. For example, you may feel more comfortable seeing yourself as a Facilitator of learning rather than a Gatekeeper, or vice versa. You could number these from 1 to 12, with 12 being what you feel most comfortable with.

After you have considered which of the functions you are more comfortable undertaking, develop your professional curiosity by answering the following questions.

- I am more comfortable with these aspects of the practice education role because…
- I am less comfortable with these aspects of the practice education role because…
- Have my thoughts about the different aspects of the role changed over time? Why? Why not?
- Does my level of comfort change depending on the characteristics of the individuals I am working with? Why? Why not?
- What if aspects of their identity such as ethnicity, gender, age, class or sexuality differ from mine? Does this make a difference to how I feel? Why? Why not?
- To become more comfortable with some of the functions of a practice educator I need to…
- Is there anything else I need to do move out of my comfort zone to ensure that I am using the legitimate authority which is inherent within the role?

To create an effective learning environment, it is important that practice educators become comfortable with the many dimensions of the role and the power contained within these or at the very least are overtly aware of which aspects they feel most at ease with.

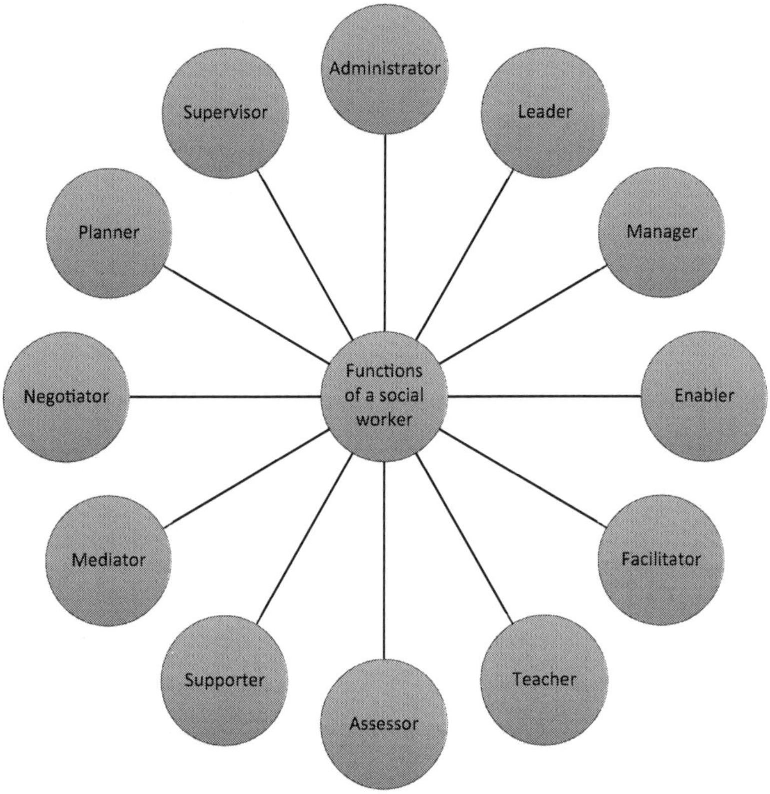

Figure 5.2 Functions of a social worker

Reflective activity for a practice educator to use with a student part 2: Position
The Position activity can be adapted by practice educators to explore how comfortable students are with the power linked to the legitimate authority they hold as a social work student. The various roles of a social worker could be discussed (see Figure 5.2) and the student asked if there are any others they feel should be added to the list. The student is then asked to number the functions from 1 to 12, with 12 being one that the student feels most comfortable with. Ideas of positional power can then be introduced using the following questions to promote a reflective discussion.

- ❖ I am more comfortable with these aspects of the social work role because...
- ❖ I am less comfortable with these aspects of the social work role because...
- ❖ To become more comfortable with some of the functions of a social worker, during this placement I need to...
- ❖ Does my level of comfort change depending on the individual characteristics of the citizens I am working with? Why? Why not?
- ❖ What if aspects of their identity such as ethnicity, gender, age, class or sexuality differ from mine? Does this make a difference to how I feel? Why? Why not?
- ❖ Is there anything I need to do in relation to this to be effective in my role as a social work student?

Part 3: Power

Figure 5.3 Reflective activity images

Reflective activity for a practice educator part 3: Power

As practice educators it is important to reflect on our own internal world because this can help us to tune in to the range of feelings and worries that a student may be experiencing (Finch, 2017). Working with students can produce a range of emotions and feelings for practice educators, particularly when working with students who may be struggling.

- Look at the images in Figure 5.3 and identify one that reflects your feelings when a student is on track to pass the practice placement.
- Now pick an image that reflects your feelings when you are working with a student and there is a possibility that they could fail the placement.
- Was it easy to find an image to represent a successful student? Why?
- Was it more difficult to identify an image that reflected a student who may be struggling? Why? Why not?
- Are you able to make any connections with how you feel about the different functions of the practice educator role?
- How does this relate to concepts of power discussed within this chapter?

When things are going well, working with students can be stimulating and immensely enjoyable and you may have identified images that represent these feelings. However, when things are going less well and the student is struggling to meet the necessary knowledge, skills and values expected, different emotions and feelings may be experienced by the practice educator, such as imposter syndrome (self-doubt), uncertainty, guilt and anger (Finch, 2017). These could also be felt by the student. However, there will always be a minority of students who will not meet the necessary requirements to enter the profession. If this is identified during the practice learning opportunity, it falls to the practice educator, after following due process, to recommend a placement failure and use the legitimate power held within their role appropriately.

Power and Rights-based (PRB) Triangle

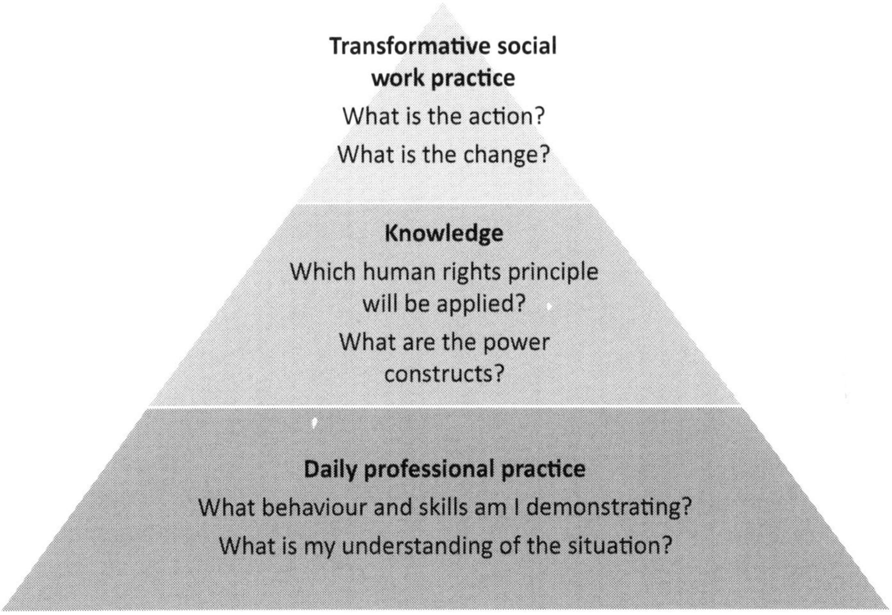

The 'social workers are heroes' narrative has always sat incredibly uncomfortably with me and this model was developed as an antithesis to that. So, instead of seeing practitioners as swooping in to 'rescue' someone as a passive recipient with a 'gift' of support, this tool was originally created for students to start to understand and work with people as having agency and being viewed as 'rights-holders' (Howells, 2019, p 163). Originally developed with domestic abuse victims/survivors in mind, the tool's aim was to bridge the more abstract ideas around people's rights and power, with steps to concretely translate these into practice. The tool is transferable across social work and has been adapted specifically for practice educators and students in this chapter.

Rights, not 'gifts' of support

First, two significant points have brought this tool together.

1. Human rights can often be seen as rhetoric and too politicised for everyday social work.
2. The role of power in social work has been understated and requires interrogation and scrutiny.

To address both points together, the **Power and Rights-based Triangle** tool can support an integration of a meaningful rights-based approach and aid a greater understanding of power differentials within a student's daily practice, moving beyond the abstract and theoretical to more practical social work. There can be a lack of clarity around power being seen as a capability (Tew, 2006) and, at times, some ambivalence around practitioners' possession of power and connection to rights within their work. This may particularly resonate with practice educators, in positions of power, alongside a learner. This is despite rights being embedded in practice education as part of an anti-oppressive and anti-discriminatory approach with students (BASW, 2019a). However, as BASW (2019b, p 23) states:

All social work is at its best when a spirit of human rights and a desire to defend or restore clients' rights is embedded in practice. Practice risks failing when human rights take second place behind process, pragmatism, tightening thresholds, expediency, resource pressures or personal moral judgements.

As such, the practice educator can draw on the **Power and Rights-based Triangle** tool to guide the student to make explicit links between their daily professional practice, focused on their behaviours and skills, helping them to operationalise their knowledge of power constructs and human rights principles through their knowledge and action.

The power of theory

The **Power and Rights-based Triangle** tool primarily draws on the different types of power (Avelino, 2021; see also Thompson, 2017, p 96), while also deriving from feminist theories and strengths-based and empowerment practices. Thompson identifies four types of power – power to, power over, power with and power from within. For ease, these have been broken down in the following way (Howells, 2021).

Power construct	How power is exercised
Power to *Empowerment*	Support provided to individual to achieve goals. Consider positionality, characteristics and privileges.
Power over *Oppression or authority*	Can be either understood as legitimate authority or built on control and subordination. Consider the impact of structural aspects.
Power with *Collaboration*	Building bridges of partnership and pulling together as a collective.
Power within *Spiritual*	Ability to draw on self-worth and self-knowledge.

The power of how

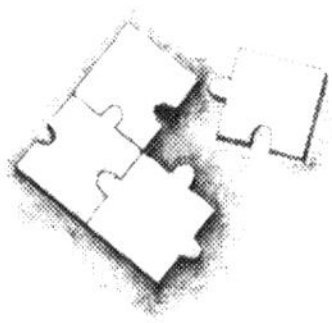

Using the **Power and Rights-based Triangle** tool, the practice educator can guide the student through the questions or areas of exploration within each of the three parts of the triangle with the student noting down their responses. These responses will form the basis of discussion within a supervision session to explore the power dynamics within a situation in further detail and consider the connection to human rights. As a development point, the practice educator could also complete this activity at the same time and both sets of responses can form the discussion, exploring the similarities and differences around the same situation. The tool can be used to deepen understanding around a piece of work that involves an individual or a situation with a professional or to explore the practice educator and student relationship itself.

1. Daily professional practice

Deconstructing the situation will help students and practice educators understand what is happening. This is where the **'sense-making'** happens. This can be addressed through consideration of the following aspects.

- Interrogating behaviours and skills will support the development of insight.
- Establishing the level of participation will lead to identifying any implicit assumptions made about the situation or individual and help develop understanding of relational and structural elements.

- Identifying the level of participation connects to power and relates to involvement, connection and reciprocity (Reynaert et al, 2021).
- Exclusionary practice will be highlighted and lead to different ways of working.

Questions to explore daily professional practice	
What is my understanding? Deconstruction of the situation	1. What is happening? 2. How might the situation be understood differently from the practice educator's or individual's perspective?
Behaviours and skills demonstrated Development of insight	1. How am I exercising power? 2. How am I participating within the situation? eg am I participating with the individual or am I expecting them to participate with me? Is the participation meaningful, inclusive with shared accountability or one-sided, tokenistic and consultative? 3. What behaviours and skills am I demonstrating? 4. What are the implicit assumptions or knowledge within the situation? Is this influencing the situation? 5. What is working well?

2. Knowledge

This section of the triangle is about strengthening the connection between **theory and practice**. Scrutinising the power constructs and making explicit links to the fundamental rights principles will support students and practitioners in two ways:

1. deepening their understanding of power differentials;
2. moving beyond what is on 'paper' and towards the 'practice' of human rights in social work.

Questions to break down the power constructs	
Power to Aspects which help to create change and achieve goals	1. How am I positioned to access power? So, what are my characteristics and/or privileges – *ethnicity, class, gender, socio-economic status, ability, sexual orientation, education and background.* 2. Where do I draw power from in terms of my social work role? eg position, professional status, organisational context, legal authority, academic qualification, knowledge and/or the state. 3. What else helps me feel empowered within this relationship?
Power over How power is exercised and possessed	1. Does the relationship feel hierarchical and imbalanced? If so, please explain. 2. Does the relationship include resistance and conflict? If so, please explain. 3. Does the relationship feel negotiated and reciprocal? If so, please explain. 4. Can you identify any structural aspects which impact the situation? eg workplace culture, bureaucratic policies and processes, management ethos. 5. Is there a difference between my interests and those of the individual or practice educator? 6. Is there a legitimate use of power through my use of authority?
Power with Greater power through collaboration	1. What are the values that I present within this relationship? eg partnership with a shared/balanced level of power with respect, mutual support and collaboration to build bridges and across difference. 2. How do I learn within this relationship?

→

Power from within Recognition of self-worth and drawing on inner strength	1. What do I have that equips me when faced with challenges? 2. What helps me to overcome obstacles?

Areas of exploration to break down the human rights principles (United Nations Human Rights, Office of the High Commissioner, nd and adapted from Androff, 2018)	
Dignity *Article 1 Free and equal* *Article 3 Right to life* *Article 4 Freedom from slavery* *Article 5 Freedom from torture* *Article 12 Right to privacy*	1. Recognition of ways that the individual has been respected, or dehumanised, stigmatised or blamed. 2. What 'lens' is being applied and how does it explain/support the situation? eg passive gifting of support or active, capable rights-holder? 3. Draw upon the Code of Ethics (BASW, 2021).
Non-discrimination *Article 2 Freedom from discrimination* *Article 6 Right to recognition before the law* *Article 7 Right to equality before the law* *Article 8 Access to justice*	1. Consideration of the protected characteristics, eg gender, age, sexual orientation, etc (see Equality and Human Rights Commission, 2021 for more information). 2. Considerations of inclusion and exclusion, including historic notions of marginalisation. 3. Ways in which practice is understood to be culturally appropriate.

Article 9 Freedom from arbitrary detention *Article 11 Presumption of innocence* *Article 14 Right to asylum* *Article 18 Freedom of religion or belief*	4. Exploration of how identity and diversity shape human experience. 5. Recognition of privilege(s).
Participation *Article 13 Freedom of movement* *Article 16 Right to marriage and to found a family* *Article 17 Right to own a property* *Article 20 Freedom of assembly* *Article 21 Right to partake in public affairs* *Article 22 Right to social security* *Article 23 Right to work* *Article 24 Right to leisure and rest* *Article 25 Right to adequate standard of living* *Article 26 Right to education* *Article 27 Right to take part in cultural, artistic and scientific life* *Article 28 Right to a free and fair world*	1. Explore ways in which the individual has influence and input into decisions which affect them. 2. Is participation tokenistic or genuine and meaningful? How have you reached this conclusion? 3. You may find Arnstein's Ladder of Citizen Participation helpful to refer to within this section (Arnstein, 1969, cited in Organizing Engagement, 2021) 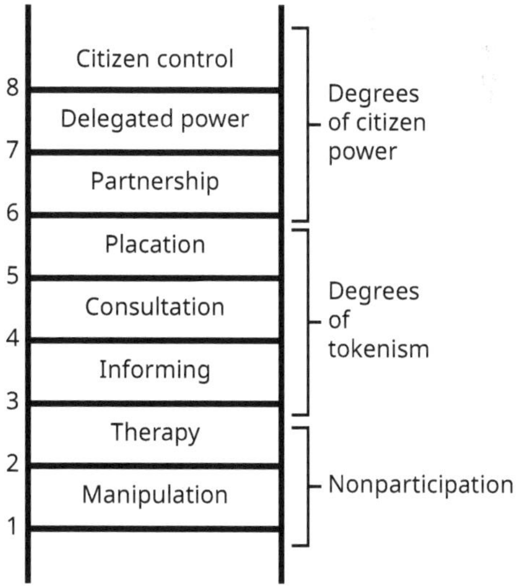

→

Transparency *Article 10 Right to a fair trial* *Article 19 Freedom of expression*	1. Consideration of processes, policies and budget transparency and the influence upon the working relationship. 2. Discussion of rationales, evidence-based decisions, assessments and judgements. 3. Implementing reflexivity and critically reflective skills.
Accountability *Article 15 Right to nationality* *Article 29 Duty to your community* *Article 30 Rights are inalienable*	1. Utilising legislation and research to enhance professional credibility. 2. Consideration of the way in which you advocate, empower and inform individuals. 3. Exploring ways in which to contribute towards a rights-based culture.

3. Transformative social work practice

The final section of the triangle helps students and practitioners to become **active agents** of human rights in their practice, supporting understanding in how to overcome barriers and address the complex nature of power within human interactions. This is significant because students and practice educators operate within a people profession, which means your actions can either reinforce feelings of powerlessness or contribute towards emancipation. As Freire (1984, p 122) points out, '*Washing one's hands of the conflict between the powerful and the powerless means to side with the powerful, not to be neutral*'. Put simply, you are either part of the solution, or part of the problem.

Questions to explore the next steps	
What is the change? What direction do you want to take?	1. What is the desired goal?
What is the action? How this will be achieved	1. How will this be achieved? 2. What do I need to move towards the intended goal? Who will help me?

The power of students

When using this tool with students, we were working through the areas of exploration to break down the human rights principles. Students were having group discussions drawing on their practice learning opportunity, particularly focusing on the 'participation' section. One student shared how the tool had helped them realise that the participation with a family was driven by an individualistic, needs-led approach and helped them to shift their actions to be more rights-based.

The power of people

To understand the power differentials in more detail this tool can be adapted to any situation. The power constructs section can be adapted to a different power theory and/or model, with some flexibility in the questions. You may also choose to do a mapping exercise of the *Articles* across the five areas of exploration with a student to identify if some cross over into more than one area. You may also find the **Power and Rights-based Triangle** tool helpful in work with people who feel powerless as a way to enhance more control within their lives by identifying different power relations and informing them of their rights. To support with deconstructing the power relations in more detail, you may find Fook's (2016, pp 137–9) comprehensive set of questions helpful in making sense of situations in more detail.

Three powerful points

1. Where there are people, there are interactions. Where there are interactions, there is power. As such, power is a central tenet of social work and more focus towards understanding its role and working constructively with power will strengthen students' and practice educators' social work practice.

2. Practice educators need to be aware of and comfortable with the power they hold as gatekeeper, assessor, mentor, supervisor, educator and role model. They need to use their legitimate authority to make the necessary recommendations regarding a student's suitability and capability to become a professional social worker.

3. The above tools help to operationalise power between a practice educator and student, supporting an understanding that power is not just negative and oppressive, but also a positive and productive force within a '*power-charged learning relationship*' (Hackett and Marsland, 1997, p 49).

References

Androff, D (2018) Practising Human Rights in Social Work: Reflections and Rights-based Approaches. *Journal of Human Rights and Social Work*, 3: 179–82.

Avelino, F (2021) Theories of Power and Social Change. Power Contestations and Their Implications for Research on Social Change and Innovation. *Journal of Political Power*, 14(3): 425–48.

British Association of Social Workers (BASW) (2019a) *BASW England Practice Educator Professional Standards for Social Work*. [online] Available at: www.basw.co.uk/system/files/resources/peps-for-social-work.pdf (accessed 20 February 2022).

British Association of Social Workers (BASW) (2019b) *Social Work and Human Rights: A Practice Guide*. [online] Available at: www.basw.co.uk/resources/social-work-and-human-rights-practice-guide (accessed 20 February 2022).

British Association of Social Workers (BASW) (2021) *The Code of Ethics for Social Work*. [online] Available at: www.basw.co.uk/about-basw/code-ethics (accessed 20 February 2022).

Equality and Human Rights Commission (2021) Protected Characteristics. [online] Available at: www.equalityhumanrights.com/en/equality-act/protected-characteristics (accessed 20 February 2022).

Field, P, Jasper, C and Littler, L (2014) *Practice Education in Social Work: Achieving Professional Standards.* Northwich: Critical Publishing.

Finch, J (2017) *Supporting Struggling Students on Placement.* Bristol: Policy Press.

Fook, J (2016) *Social Work: A Critical Approach to Practice.* 3rd ed. London: Sage.

Freire, P (1984) *The Politics of Education: Culture, Power and Liberation*. Westport, MA: Bergin & Garvey Publisher Inc.

French, J and Raven, B (1959) The Bases of Social Power. In Cartwright, D and Zander, A (eds) *Group Dynamics: Research and Theory* (pp 259–69). New York: Harper and Row.

Hackett, S and Marsland, P (1997) Perceptions of Power: An Exploration of the Dynamics in the Student–Tutor–Practice Teacher Relationships within Child Protection Placements. *Social Work Education*, 16(2): 44–62.

Howells, A (2019) IDEAS, Domestic Abuse and Social Work. In Dix, H, Hollinrake, S and Meade, J (eds) *Relationship-based Social Work with Adults* (pp 157–72). St Albans: Critical Publishing.

Howells, A (2021) Rights, Not 'Gifts' of Support in Statutory Social Work. Poster presentation at *4th European Conference on Domestic Violence*. Slovenia, online, 13–15 September 2021.

Organizing Engagement (2021) Ladder of Citizen Participation. [online] Available at: https://organizingengagement.org/models/ladder-of-citizen-participation (accessed 20 February 2022).

Reynaert, D, Nachtergaele, S, De Stercke, N, Gobeyn, H and Roose, R (2021) Social Work as a Human Rights Profession: An Action Framework. *The British Journal of Social Work*, 20210503. doi:10.1093/bjsw/bcab083

Tew, J (2006) Understanding Power and Powerlessness: Towards a Framework for Emancipatory Practice in Social Work. *Journal of Social Work*, 6(1): 33–51.

Thompson, N (2017) *Theorizing Practice*. 2nd ed. London: Palgrave Macmillan.

Thompson, N (2018) *Promoting Equality*. 4th ed. London: Palgrave Macmillan.

United Nations Human Rights Office of the High Commissioner (nd) Universal Declaration of Human Rights. [online] Available at: www.standup4humanrights.org/en/declaration.html (accessed 20 February 2022).

Brush on that daily smile

Angela Bell

Unlock the regular happiness
Keep those corners raised.
Into the urban wilderness
where faceless eyes are glazed.

Brush on that daily smile.

Climb the pit of grief each day
to face new fights with fears.
Memories that just won't fade
of beeps and wires and tears.

Brush on that daily smile.

Telephones ring, voices chatter
for now, the pain feels numb;
Caught in noisy office banter
knowing the ache will come.

Brush on that daily smile.

Alone in bed, lamp stays on
I dare not close my eyes,
For if I do, I'll see her there
vacant and empty. I cry.

Brush on that daily smile.

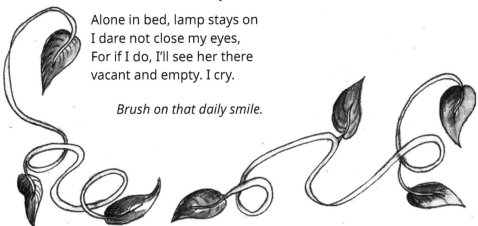

Chapter 6

The Musician, 'The Stripper' and The Boxing Day Flood: The use of stories in social work

Alison Taylor

Introduction

Human beings are storytellers by nature. From myths to fairy tales and anecdotes, telling stories is a fundamental aspect of human experience. After all, who does not love listening to a story or even have a story to tell? Embedded in our social fabric, stories draw us to them for many reasons. Social work, by its very nature, focuses on the detail of people's lives. Put simply, stories offer insight to the world making meaning and helping to make sense of people's lives. Some stories might include facts or more abstract concepts, or perhaps share personal experiences and historic events, all of which can spark our curiosity and capture our attention. As such, storytelling practices are inherent to the profession and this chapter supports an emphasis towards social work as fundamentally a *'narrative activity'* (Baldwin, 2013, p 3). However, our narratives do not operate in a vacuum and context plays a role in the way in which we story our lives and the meanings that are formed. With these ideas about story in mind, this chapter's context starts with our storyteller, me, Alison. I am a mother to a child with autism and I am going to tell you a few different stories and show you how, as practice educators, you can use these narrative tools with students to build confidence, self-esteem and self-efficacy linked to well-being.

So let us begin…

Imagine if you will that I am your favourite auntie, and you are now sitting in my house in a comfy armchair with a mug of hot steaming tea in your hand and a warm snuggly blanket across your legs. It is a bit stormy outside and so being in the comfort of a warm family home reassures you that everything is right with the world.

This is a huge relief as it has just been one of those weeks. In fact, it has been one of those months… or maybe even years… You, as my relative, are a social worker and we both know that you cannot share the details of your work, but you can share how you feel about the things you see and the tools that you have to get through life. I want you to not just survive but to feel that you are coping, maybe even that you are thriving in your life.

As well as being your auntie, I am also a carer of your cousin who has very significant autism. I have been part of a team working in the local university helping to share the life of a carer with social work students. On top of that I have a master's degree in applied positive psychology and coaching psychology with an interest in resilience. Because of this, we always have very lively discussions and spend hours putting the world of social work 'to rights'.

So here we are… no place to go… Nothing to do… Just to be…

'How are you?' I ask.

Now you know that the question is one of genuine concern that doesn't expect a response of 'fine thanks!' Anyway, even if you did say 'fine, thank you' you know that I would not let you get away with that, so you exhale slowly and begin the story. I listen intently without interrupting and you inwardly note that the chance to share without interruption is so rare – in fact, it never happens other than here.

You talk about how you are tired in your role, how heavy the workload is and how unappreciated you feel.

'The Stripper' story

I listen carefully as you describe how your week has been… and then I lean back in my chair and reach over and take your hand. I begin my first story… you know that my son Fabian is great at playing the piano. In fact, no one taught him how to play; he just sat down one day and played. He was watching his sister painstakingly trying to pick out the notes of a tune on the piano and then he waited for her to get up from the piano stool. He then went and sat down at the stool and played the piece with both hands. You see, it is hard being a child with additional needs when your older sister is good at so many things. So, when you see her finding something hard and you know you can do it, it becomes sweet justice to just go over, take a seat and play the piece with ease. After that he set his sights on being an organist.

When my son was younger, the church that we attended had a service for older members of the community three times a year. It was Fabian's joy and privilege to be able to be the organist for this service. In the week before the Easter service, my son kept teasing me, saying he was going to play the wrong music at the service. I thought he was joking, but he kept on with it. The Easter service is quite sombre and, as the vicar announced the second hymn, I saw Fabian chuckle to himself. Then, instead of playing the hymn 'Amazing Grace', I could hear him strike up the opening chords of a completely different tune. To my absolute horror, I recognised the opening bars of 'The Stripper'! I took hold of his hands and said, 'No, play the hymn'. I let go of his hands and again he started to play 'The Stripper'. I took his hands again and said, 'Last chance'. I could see the congregation of older people who had struggled to their feet to sing patiently waiting. Once again, he played the opening bars of 'The Stripper'. I just wanted the ground to open up and swallow me in that moment; I was so embarrassed. There was a complete hush in the church and the vicar was looking at us wondering what was happening. I turned to Fabian and told him that he was going home with his dad and that I would play for the rest of the service.

Later in the day (after I had calmed down a bit), I asked Fabian why he had done that. For the first time in his life, he told me the reason. Six days earlier, I had refused to park my car in the place that he had requested. So, he had 'kept his powder dry' for six days and then unleashed his revenge in public. However, instead of being angry about this, I saw an opportunity. 'I understand that you were angry with me over the parking', I said, 'but you took it out on everyone in the church. The people who came for a service had to wait while you played the wrong thing; the vicar may well have felt embarrassed too. Was that fair?' His face fell as he realised what he had done, and again that day I realised that there was another first. I also realised that his choice of music had been because of its complete inappropriateness for the occasion. I realised that he knew what appropriate and inappropriate meant. So, we had a conversation about this too. Suddenly, I realised that what had been an excruciatingly embarrassing afternoon was not so bad after all. In fact, nobody died, and most people were laughing about it. It became a bit of a joke to see who knew which tune it was that Fabian was playing.

So, the reason I am telling this story is that it is not so much what happens in our lives that determines our experience, but what we think about what happens that makes the difference to how we feel. It is the meaning that we attribute to events that makes us resilient to challenges. We can construct ***'The Stripper' Story*** *as 'I can't trust Fabian not to do something completely inappropriate' or, this was my chance to teach him something so that he can be more successful in future. I cannot control what my son chooses to do, but I am totally in control of where I go next in my thinking about it. Something that starts out as a challenge can then become a gift as a child with difficulties has an opportunity to learn something that will help him to be more successful in future. So, in light of this, I have some 'go to' mantras that I can draw on when life (or Fabian) throws me a curve ball that I want to share with you. These are things like the following:*

- *I am making a difference in my life and the life of my child;*
- *I am treading down the path so that others who follow me will have a guide and an easier path going forwards;*
- *I am the best person to help my son because a) I love him, b) I will love him for all his life, c) I know more about him than anyone else on the planet;*
- *If no one else can see what I am doing, I will acknowledge it as valuable as I am the one who defines my value and the value of what I am doing;*

Being able to imagine myself into the future and see a time when all my efforts have paid off helps to make meaningful mantras. You see, when things are hard and we feel unappreciated, there is always a way to fill our own cup and to define our own value or give ourselves that sense of purpose with our actions. We don't need others to value what we do in order for it to have value. This applies to everyone, including social workers and social work students.

Theory

Reframing is a skill commonly used in brief therapies such as motivational interviewing (Miller and Rollnick, 2013) to draw out and highlight an individual's strengths and successes. It is a way to build resilience by enhancing cognitive flexibility to create a positive adaptation to adversity. It works by helping the person to master their own thought processes by understanding that there is more than one way to view an event. The story above is an example of this as I could decide that **'The Stripper' Story** was the most embarrassing moment of my entire life or a brilliant opportunity to teach my son how to be more successful in future. If this event hadn't happened, I would not have had the chance to teach this lesson so effectively.

To make this theory relevant to our life we need to sort out what is fact and observation (Fabian played 'The Stripper' tune in church) from my interpretation of it (I'm embarrassed because people will judge what he did, or this is a great opportunity to teach him something that will help him to be more successful in future). Each of the two thoughts will result in my experiencing different feelings. So, it is not so much the things that happen to us in our life; it is our interpretation that affects how we feel. As my interpretation of the event is a belief and not a fact, it can be changed.

How to use the story, part 1

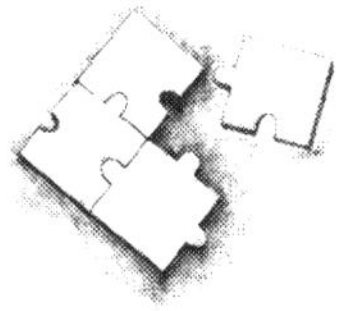

Practice educators could ask a student to read the experience outlined above and use this as a basis to discuss how reframing a situation can have a powerful impact. They could then relate their thoughts to an experience of their own.

What happened? (fact/ observation)	My interpret-ation (these are not facts)	My feelings are:	Another alternative interpretation (these are not facts)	My feelings would be:

Put simply, the learning from this activity for the student is that we, as individuals, are in charge of our experience because we can decide what frame to apply to any circumstance. This not only helps students with holding different explanations in mind about the one situation; it also helps when things might not go the way we want them to, where understanding and meaning can be seen through different lenses, perhaps some with more of a positive spin to them.

This can then lead into the 'best possible or ideal self' exercise, which is a research-backed positive psychology intervention designed to increase optimism and hope. All of us dream of situations where we perform at our best. This daydream serves to create a vision of a preferred life that can be aspired to. The more specificity that the dream has, the more useful this activity can be. By clearly imagining a future ideal self, the easier it is to create goals that can then be worked towards. A clear picture of that life can motivate us to strive towards that goal (Biswas-Diener, 2010).

How to use the story, part 2

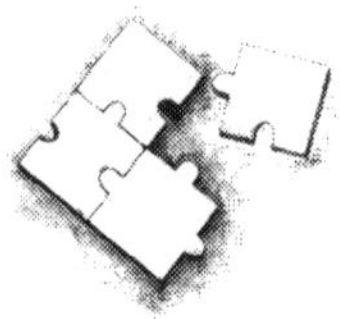

This additional reflective activity can be used effectively to help students to consider and visualise their '*preferred future*' (Iveson, 1994).

As a practice educator, ask the student to spend 15 minutes of their reflective time each day for four consecutive days to write about the following.

Imagine a time, five years from now, when everything that you hope for now has been accomplished. Try to be as specific as you can and write about what your life will be like. Try not to censor yourself as you write. This is about you being your best self. Consider your career, your academic work, relationships, finances, family, friends and anything else that is important to you. Be as specific as you can – the more detail the better.

You could also use these coaching questions (Biswas-Diener, 2010) to help the student to gain more from the exercise.

- How important is it to you to achieve the 'ideal self'?
- When are you planning to make the changes associated with achieving the 'ideal self'?
- What resources and opportunities do you have that will help you work towards your 'ideal self'?

- What hurdles do you anticipate? How can these be part of the growth process?
- What factors inform your vision of your 'ideal self'?
- How internal (as opposed to external) are the values that inform your 'ideal self'?
- What person, living or dead, is similar to your 'ideal self'?
- Name a single small behaviour you can change as a first step towards your 'ideal self'.
- How can you chart your progress towards your 'ideal self'?

Now back to the storytelling...

I can see that you are processing this new idea and how it could work to improve things. I pause to give you space to think. Finally, you sigh and say, 'I always wondered how you managed to be so patient, Auntie'.

Well then let me tell you another story....

The Boxing Day Story

There was one year, just after we had completed a lot of building work on the house. It was Boxing Day and the family were watching an afternoon film on the TV. Fabian wasn't interested in the film, so he was playing quietly in his bedroom – or so we thought.

Suddenly, the lights went off and the TV went off, and we could hear shrieking coming from upstairs. Then there was an almighty crash as a ceiling fell in. I rushed upstairs to find my son. He was standing in the bathroom ankle deep in water with a large lemonade bottle in his hand. He had been filling the bottle from the bath tap and then tipping it onto the floor. Immediately, I realised what the crash was and also just how much water he had poured onto the floor, which had now rendered the house uninhabitable – on Boxing Day.

*When I tell **The Boxing Day Story**, it is usually met first with a stunned silence, followed by comments along the lines of how patient I must be to have dealt with that scenario. However, if you do not judge the event as bad, then there is nothing to be patient with. There is work to do to clean up and repair for sure but calling it 'bad' does not fix it; it just adds to the load. I am sure that Fabian was enjoying playing with the water. I do not suppose for a minute that he intended to trash the house. He was doing his best to amuse himself on an afternoon that was out of his normal routine. Cutting the slack for others has two benefits. On top of only having to tend to the aftermath of the flood, it meant that I didn't have to clean up while carrying angry feelings. It meant that I could give all of my energy to discussing with others how to prevent this happening again. The solution was to change my son's bedroom to the room underneath the bathroom – which was my daughter's suggestion. Now he knew the consequences of playing with water, he wouldn't risk his own stuff getting damaged and so wouldn't do it again. Additionally, if we are in the habit of not judging others it is easier to cut ourselves some slack too. I could have given myself a hard time judging myself for not supervising him adequately that afternoon. I could have totally taken all the blame onto myself for that event. However, I do not need judgement as a moral compass to tell me what I should do. I could decide that I need to be with him more because I want him to be safe and because he is fun to be with. By dropping judgements, it gets rid of all the mental chatter that gets in the way of problem solving.*

Theory

The broaden-and-build theory (Fredrickson and Joiner, 2002) suggests that new thought repertoires come from feeling positive emotions. We are all very familiar with the idea that negative emotions like fear lead to reactions such as fight, flight, freeze or fawn, all of which prevent us from thinking flexibly. What the broaden-and-build theory articulates is what happens when positive emotions are felt, which is that thought patterns become more flexible and creative, which may enable novel ways to think, feel and behave. This can be useful in solving problems. As Henry Ford said, '*If you do what you've always done, you will get what you always got*'. If you are in a tight spot, then what is needed is something different. Therefore, by experiencing positive emotions we are more able to be resourceful in trying something new in resolving our difficulties.

How to use the story

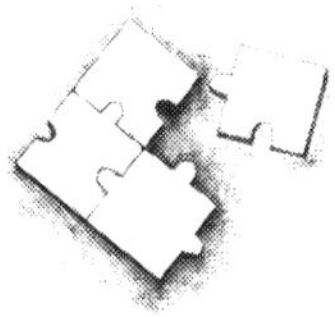

As with the first story, a practice educator could ask a student to read **The Boxing Day Story** and suggest a piece of their reflective time is used to write about something that happened during their practice learning opportunity that did not go the way they had planned, or which had taken them by surprise. They need to be prepared to share this within their next supervision. During the session, ask the student to take a pen and highlight the judgements they made about themselves. These may be things where the student has used words such as 'like', 'should have', 'must do', 'need to', 'right/wrong', 'appropriate/inappropriate', and 'good/bad'.

Then ask the student to consider how judging the event serves them – what are they wanting to achieve? Once you uncover the role of the judgement, you can find another way to achieve the things that you want by framing these in a more positive way. The last part of the exercise can be to ask the student to consider what difference it makes for them to be kinder to themselves and to consider reflecting without judgement or blame.

You may wish to ask the student to start with something small and then build up to consider bigger things. Remind the student not to judge the judgement but just take the time to understand themselves through this exercise.

And back to the storytelling...

'That's brilliant', you said, 'I can see how not judging something makes it so much easier to deal with life, using energy and ease rather than anger, upset and discomfort. What I don't see is how you stop yourself going down the rabbit hole of thinking that things that are catastrophic will never change'.

The Musician Story

Well, there is another story that I can tell you that will show you what I mean. Way back now, you will remember that we home schooled Fabian using a therapy programme. Part of that programme involved deciding that whatever he decided to do had meaning, purpose and value even if I didn't know what that was. It also showed him that I valued his choices and that there was nowhere that he could choose to go where I would not want to go with him. To do this though, I needed to be present in the moment and to focus completely on his activity so I could closely follow what he was doing. In the early days of the programme, he would walk in circles around the edge of the room writing in the air with his finger. This activity went on for weeks if not months. As I wanted to connect with him and to encourage him to play with me, I did the same thing as him. This was more than just copying; it was a sincere attempt to join in with his game. It was a way to find out what his motivations were because he couldn't tell me at the time.

One night after spending most of the day doing this activity, I decided to take a long hot bath. While lying there in the water my thoughts drifted to a band rehearsal that I had recently been to, where we listened to a new song that we were going to learn. As I was recalling the song, I realised that I was writing in the air in the same way as I had been doing all day with Fabian. Then I wondered, 'but what if he is walking around thinking about music all day too?'

So, the next day, I was walking with Fabian around in circles writing in the air. This time though I started to put notes to his movements and to make a tune. Before too long, I realised the tune – it was Tchaikovsky's 1812 overture. My son went on to become an accomplished pianist and I think that all those months spent walking around the room allowed him to build the gross motor patterns that he then called on to play the piano from scratch. Playing the piano has given him a social role in groups as 'Mr Music Man'. It has been something that he is good at and has given his self-esteem a massive boost. All of this would not have happened if we had not been present and stayed with him when he was doing something that I didn't understand. If I had been concerned in those days about whether he might one day live independently or focused on all of the things he couldn't do, I would have missed the thing he actually could do. This is the lesson of mindfulness.

Theory

Mindfulness has been used as a therapeutic intervention within areas of social work practice such as mental health for some time. However, through the recognition that professionals such as social workers can experience vicarious trauma or secondary trauma, mindfulness is being used to support well-being as it teaches us to pay attention on purpose to the present moment. It is said that the past is history, the future is a mystery, and all we have is this present moment, which is why it is called the present because it is a gift (Kabat-Zinn, 1994). Being in the present moment relieves us of regret from the past and stress about the future. It is the ultimate example of having nowhere to go, nothing to do, just to be and enjoy whatever this moment brings. By doing so, this lessens the pressure on us in each moment when we can learn to control our thinking rather than letting it control us.

There is a tradition that Tibetan Buddhist monks follow to create wonderful mandalas in the sand using brightly coloured paints or mosaic pieces. These mandalas are laborious to create and can take hours, days or even weeks to complete. After they are complete, they pray over the mandala and then destroy it and pour the sand into the nearest living form of water such as a river or the sea. It serves as a reminder to savour each moment as nothing is permanent; it is also a reminder to create beauty in each moment.

How to use the story

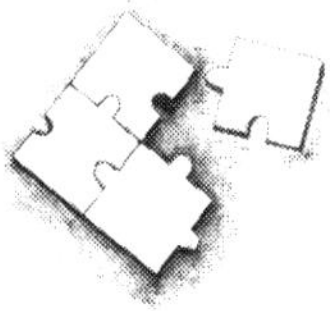

The practice educator and student can read **The Musician Story** together to promote a discussion about the need to be present within social work, as well as part of self-care. Mindfulness is a skill which needs to be practised and the following activity is one example of the different ways this can be achieved.

Activity

This exercise can be used as part of supervision or the student could be asked to do this as a personal activity during their reflective time.

Gather some inexpensive craft materials or ask the student to find some bits and pieces that they can use to make something of beauty. Some suggestions are to download a mandala to colour or use some paints to create a picture. Ask the student to completely immerse themselves in the process of creation, knowing that whatever they make is for this moment only and more for the experience of creation rather than for the outcome. Suggest to the student that if they find their mind drifting onto other things, to gently, without judgement, come back to the activity. Mindfulness is not something we can do straight away; that is why it is known as a practice.

Then, when the piece has been created, ask the student to destroy it and reflect on the experience, either individually or in supervision with you, by considering the following questions.

- How did it feel to create something impermanent?
- How did you feel destroying it?
- What difference do you think this activity might make to how you view events during your working day?
- Who are you letting decide your value?
- Who decides how valuable what you do is?
- What connections can you make to your social work practice?

Three key points

1. The thoughts that we have about events do not represent facts; they just represent the lens that we choose to see an event through. This is good news because if they are not facts, we can change them in a way that helps us to become more resilient practitioners.
2. When reflecting on things that have happened, if we can review them without judgement, it makes it easier to think of new ways to deal with a situation. This gives us a greater chance of success as well as a more pleasurable experience of the review.

3. Mindfulness helps us to become aware of how much power we have to choose our own thoughts. It gives us skills that enable us to focus wholeheartedly on positive thoughts while noting and letting pass thoughts that are not useful to the present moment, and therefore it supports our well-being.

References

Baldwin, C (2013) *Narrative Social Work Theory and Application*. Bristol: Policy Press.

Biswas-Diener, R (2010) *Practicing Positive Psychology: Assessment, Activities, and Strategies for Success*. Hoboken, NJ: John Wiley & Sons.

Fredrickson, B L and Joiner, T (2002) Positive Emotions Trigger Upward Spirals Toward Emotional Wellbeing. *Psychological Science*, 13(2): 172–5.

Iveson, C (1994) Preferred Futures, Exceptional Pasts. Presentation to the European Brief Therapy Association Conference, Stockholm. In Shennan, G (2019) *Solution-Focused Practice: Effective Communication to Facilitate Change*. 2nd ed. London: Red Globe.

Kabat-Zinn, J (1994) *Wherever You Go, There You Are: Mindfulness Meditation for Everyday Life.* London: Piatkus.

Miller, W and Rollnick, S (2013) *Motivational Interviewing, Helping People Change*. New York: The Guilford Press.

Chapter 7

Exploring professional curiosity and social work practice education

Nora Duckett

Introduction

This chapter looks at how 'professional curiosity' can support the process, purpose and content of practice education and student learning. It starts by considering how 'professional curiosity' is understood from psychological, sociological and practice perspectives, particularly in relation to risk assessment and decision making, and then looks at what this knowledge offers the social work practice education relationship and process. It introduces practical methods as creative tools for encouraging and increasing the likelihood of professional curiosity supporting the establishment of a productive practice education relationship, as well as explicitly informing the development and assessment of professional practice capability.

Curiosity and professional curiosity

There is no single definition of curiosity; it can be understood in different ways depending on the perspective being taken. From a psychological perspective, curiosity is seen as a basic drive for information, motivated by *'a cognitive induced deprivation that arises from the perception of a gap in knowledge and understanding'* (Loewenstein, 1994, cited in Kidd and Hayden, 2015, p 450). Also, the amount of information gained to fill the knowledge gap is thought to increase or reduce curiosity. A further consideration is the value of the information to the person seeking it, which is likened to hunger being a motivation for eating (Loewenstein, 1994). Further evidence for this idea is found in Kang et al's (2009) study of decision making about a trivia task which found participants were least curious either when they no idea about the task or when they were extremely confident about it. Interestingly, when participants had some idea, but lacked confidence, they appeared to show greater curiosity and this could apply to many social work students within their practice learning opportunity.

From a sociological standpoint, Ball (2012) argues that curiosity has multiple meanings, and its conceptualisation reflects historical and political developments, scientific paradigms and philosophical traditions. For example, over time curiosity has been distinguished as both a vice and a virtue, celebrated and something to be discouraged, and that it reduces our ability to look for non-normative explanations. One example of how curiosity is celebrated is in how it is associated with genius, like physicist Albert Einstein (1952) who said '*I have no special talent. I am only passionately curious*'. Yet from a religious perspective, according to Mother Teresa of Calcutta (nd), avoiding curiosity is seen as a way of achieving humility. The above indicates that curiosity cannot be understood outside of an appreciation of the social, political and religious contexts of the time.

Like curiosity, professional curiosity lacks a clear definition, although contexts and environments which can facilitate or decrease curiosity are emphasised in the literature. Professional curiosity is often linked to the term 'respectful uncertainty' (Laming, 2003, p 205), which is equated with keeping an open mind and involving '*the critical evaluation of information*'. From a health perspective, Price Williams and Chisholm (2018) report that a lack of curiosity increases risk for children in care, specifically when stereotypes and assumptions are left unchecked. Professional curiosity can also increase effectiveness in teaching, leadership, interprofessional relationships and organisational performance because it fosters more open communication, reduces group conflict and leads to fewer decision-making errors. People are '*less likely to look for answers that support their views [confirmation bias] or entertain stereotypes, when they are open to alternative solutions*' (Barton, 2019, p 439). Serious case reviews and safeguarding adults reviews have pointed out that a lack of professional curiosity is linked to poor assessments of risk and poor co-ordination of support. Thacker et al (2019) acknowledge that to improve professional curiosity, attention needs to be focused on organisational contexts and interprofessional collaboration. From a children's social work perspective, Burton and Revell (2017) also highlight the interdependent relationship between professional curiosity and the organisational, political and socio-economic context. They see professional curiosity as potentially transformative while at the same time something that can provoke deep anxiety in a worker given the emotional dimension of complicated relational practice dynamics, which can lead to distortion, uncertainty and confusion. Burton and Revell (2017) point out that this is rarely acknowledged in wider discussion and within serious case reviews.

The above literature indicates that to develop as a professional curious practitioner, not only do workers need psychological and sociological understandings, but they also need to develop a critical lens, that is, being explicitly and actively aware of social injustice. 'Critical curiosity', a term associated with Paulo Freire (1970), is about developing critical consciousness and a desire to learn about and combat social justice issues. Freire points to the responsibility of educators (including pedagogic social workers) to become the people who change society by recognising and overcoming oppression. For Freire, enhancing critical curiosity is part of an emancipatory project. Conceptualising professional curiosity as 'critical' enhances its worth by locating it alongside critical social work ideals, which are defined by a commitment to emancipation and transformation (Healy, 2000; Webb, 2019), particularly in relation to systematic and structural forms of inequality, marginalisation, exclusion and discrimination. Fook (2019) considers critical social work as including critical reflection and reflexive practice, and that a necessary condition of both is an awareness of the capillary nature of power, as well as understanding and engaging in power in structural terms.

Practice education and professional curiosity

There are aspects of practice education that are particularly associated with developing professionally curious professionals. The first is the relationship between the student social worker and the practice educator, which should be open, honest and trusting, as it is this quality of relationship that promotes and enables exploration of a range of possible explanations for a particular personal/professional perspective, as well as socially situated problem, concern or risk situation. Practice educators are expected to establish effective collaborative working relationships, skilfully managing the power and authority in their role, and create reflective spaces for learners' growth and development, and to enable informed professional judgements to be made about students' needs and capabilities. Honesty and openness can take time to establish and involve courage and an ability to be vulnerable, which may be at the heart of new learning (Brown, 2010).

Professional curiosity is thought to be useful so as not to take things at face value, to understand where there are gaps in knowledge and to identify discrepancies, while at the same time developing trust and maintaining a healthy scepticism and what Mason (2017) refers to as 'critical reverence', particularly where power and status differences are in evidence. It is this set of qualities that can be explicitly acknowledged, developed and modelled in the practice education supervisory relationship.

The tools below have been designed based on a checklist approach as this can be an accessible way, as part of supervision, to generate conversation and encourage a deeper look at what the answers represent and how they might enable the users of the tool to consider ideas not previously thought. The first checklist is specifically about assumptions that might be at play in the practice educator/student relationship. The second checklist is a way of encouraging the practice of professional curiosity, and the third is to acknowledge the organisational context and how this can be addressed to develop critical professional curiosity.

Assumptions Checklist

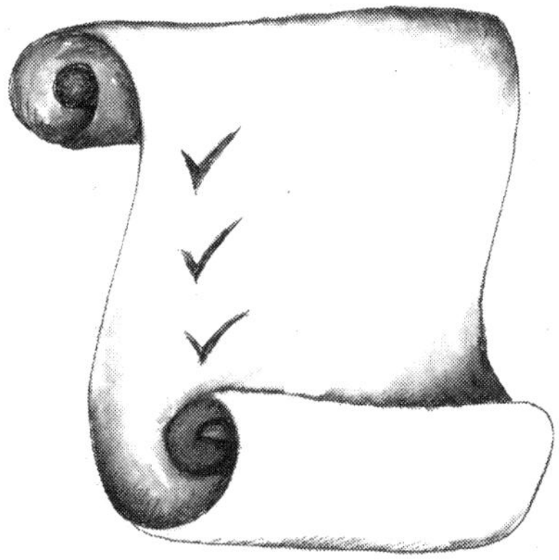

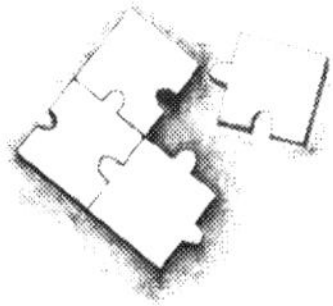

The following **Assumptions Checklist** is a table of questions which can be used as a tool to explore both the practice educator's and the student's curiosity outlook, in the context of supervision, and help develop mutual respect, appreciation and understanding. Practice educators are tasked to support students to consider different perspectives and hold different explanations in mind, using evidence to inform decisions reflecting the development of a professionally curious mindset. This tool is designed to show the assumptions we make about others and what this might mean. It allows for the practice educator and student to ask questions of each other and there is no need for the person who the questions are about to provide the accurate answer, unless you wish to do so. If you find it awkward to answer the questions, this is something to reflect on; for example, why does it feel awkward and what links can be made to the judgements we make about the people with whom we work, and to developing curiosity? Finding and using alternative questions may be preferable depending on the nature of the relationship and what has already been shared and is known about each other.

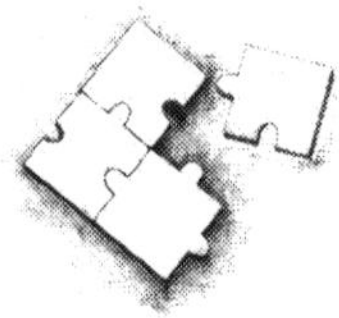

Theory and research lets us know that we are constantly making assumptions, particularly about people we don't know that well and because in making judgements we draw on fast thinking, which is highly fallible to error and bias (Kahneman, 2012). The tool is designed to acknowledge, externalise and work with assumptions, as opposed to thinking it possible to stop making them. Further impetus for this activity is rooted in how practice educators need to accept and respect students' circumstances and understand how these impact on the learning and assessment process. Practice educators and supervisors should recognise and build on students' and other learners' strengths and consider individual learning styles and a range of assessment methods.

The optimum context for this exercise to work well is for it to take place within a supportive and open professional relationship. If unacknowledged power positions are taken, and there is a tendency towards defensiveness, in these circumstances it is unlikely that this exercise will prove beneficial. Ask yourself: am I open to hearing what this person assumes about me? Some of it might be 'spot on', and some might be 'way off the mark' but it is not the benefit of the exercise to get it right. What it has the potential to do is to provide an opportunity for discussion, mutual learning and self-awareness.

The personal anecdote below helps to illustrate that asking questions about assumptions can potentially create a shift in the quality of professional relationships and communication.

A colleague repeatedly explained their ideas about a particular approach to social work. Sometimes they used different language and said it in different ways and in different contexts, but essentially it was the same message. I began to question why this kept being repeated as even though I shared their perspective to a degree, it was as if they didn't or couldn't see that I might feel similarly and therefore needed to constantly impress on me their viewpoint. During a moment when we were on our own and chatting in a relaxed, informal way, I said something like 'I am interested in how you see me because often you say [xxxx] and this makes me wonder what you think of my views and beliefs, and if you think that I do not share your perspective?' There was an initial awkwardness and then the person said, 'that's a funny question to ask' and then, 'well, I don't really want to say what I think as I don't want to insult you'. I tried to reassure the person by saying I wouldn't take it personally and would genuinely like to know their views. In this way I gave permission for it to be shared. What transpired was a more open dialogue and a sharing of mutual assumptions, which led to greater understanding and an improved working relationship.

The **Assumptions Checklist** can guide the discussion between practice educator and student.

Question (to ask of each other)	**Answer**
1. What kinds of music do I like?	
2. What is my favourite colour?	
3. Which political party do I affiliate to?	
4. What kinds of films do I enjoy watching?	
5. What is my social class?	
6. What kinds of books do I enjoy reading?	
7. Do I prefer the country or the city?	
8. How old am I?	
9. Do I observe a religious doctrine?	
10. Am I trans or cis gender?	
11. What hobbies do I have?	
12. Was I brought up in care?	
13. Do I prefer dogs, cats or neither?	
14. Do I enjoy sporting activities?	
15. Do I watch television?	
16. Do I celebrate Christmas?	
17. How many countries have I visited?	
18. Was I born in the UK?	
19. Which newspapers do I read?	
20. What is my favourite type of food?	

Professional Curiosity Self-assessment Checklist

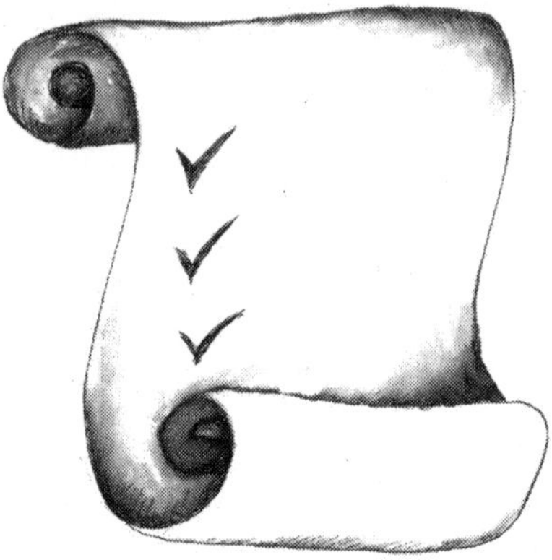

There are many examples from the literature, in analyses of serious case reviews and research into experiences of child abuse, practice responses and outcomes, indicating where opportunities for professional curiosity existed and were missed. Allnock and Miller (2013), for example, spoke with 60 young people aged 18–24 years who had experienced childhood abuse and violence and over 80 per cent said that they tried to tell someone about the abuse, but this wasn't followed up. Munro (1999) looked at 45 serious case reviews of child abuse and found that in ten cases, social workers sought the child's views, and in seven of the ten children said abuse was not happening, which was erroneously accepted, while in three of the ten, children said abuse was taking place, but they were not believed.

Ferguson's (2016) ethnographic study is interesting in that it found children were rendered invisible to social workers who were otherwise considered capable and skilled. What this indicates is that social workers, like other professionals, are not only fallible but that good practice, and what it is to be a capable practitioner, cannot be understood outside of the context (organisationally and, in a wider sense, systemically) in which the practice takes place and the subjectivity of the worker. Professional curiosity operates at this level and invites professionals to curiously interrogate their own practice, as well as other professionals' practice and the environments, contexts, experiences and testimonies of children and adults who may be at risk of harm. Understanding and recognising the dynamic interplay between psychological and organisational factors in professional networks, 'professional dangerousness', which exacerbates risk (Davies and Duckett, 2016), has the potential to support professionals' analyses and decision making. Practice education is a key learning opportunity where practice educators have the potential to inculcate a professionally curious mindset.

A further personal anecdote is shared to help indicate how professional curiosity can be about developing healthy scepticism and critical reverence (Mason, 2017), especially in the face of perceived or actual power differences.

As a Newly Qualified Social Worker I was asked by a team manager to assess a kinship care arrangement. I was told it was a standard review and would involve a brief visit to check the arrangement between a mother of five children whose youngest child, aged around six years, had undiagnosed attention deficit hyperactivity, and her close friend, who was caring for the child to give the mother a break. When I arrived, the child was inconsolable; he was expecting his mother, not me, and was deeply disappointed. His degree of emotional dysregulation, alongside the carer's tendency to minimise it, led me to ask more questions and I discovered that the child's mother had not arrived on several occasions when he had expected her to. I eventually found out that the mother had lapsed into heroin use and was unable to keep appointments. In the end I worked with this family for over five years. I learned that how a situation that is framed by someone with authority (team manager) may not be an accurate portrayal and that a professional social worker needs to follow up on her intuition and empirical observations with thorough enquiries.

Using this tool supports the development of professional curiosity through recognition of the indicators, support and obstacles in social work practice.

Beliefs about my professional curiosity	**Yes? No? Maybe?**	**Indicator**	**What helps me to achieve this?**	**What gets in the way?**
I am curious and inquisitive about what I see, hear, think and feel and about what appears to be missing.		• Aware when assumptions are being made so as not to act on them. • Actively listen and make connections.		

→

Beliefs about my professional curiosity	**Yes? No? Maybe?**	**Indicator**	**What helps me to achieve this?**	**What gets in the way?**
		• Take a holistic approach. • Aware of inconsistencies.		
I try to understand the context, process and content of information I receive.		• Explore ideas and reflect on information. • Do not take things at face value. • See social situations as complex.		
I look for new information that may disconfirm my initial views about situations, particularly where there is identified risk.		• Aware that I make mistakes. • Inform others, and apologise when mistakes are made. • Enjoy learning. • Open to feedback. • Avoid the use of blame.		
I am prepared to change my mind about a person or situation.		• Accept that things are uncertain. • Open to new information. • Manage anxieties well.		
I acknowledge my power and privilege.		• Recognise, discuss and challenge 'isms', eg racism, sexism, ageism, disablism, childism, classism, heterosexism.		

Beliefs about my professional curiosity	Yes? No? Maybe?	Indicator	What helps me to achieve this?	What gets in the way?
I am healthily sceptical about the things I read and hear.		• Look for inconsistencies. • Look for alternative perspectives.		
I respectfully challenge people's ideas if I disagree with or am unsure about them.		• Aware of conflict avoidance and unconscious bias.		
I think critic-ally about cul-tural contexts and try to make what is implicit explicit.		• Aware of cultural relativism. • Understand culture as tacit. • Aware of professional dangerousness.		
I talk to influential others about concerns and questions about practice.		• Reflect with others who help me to see different perspectives and who provoke deeper thinking.		

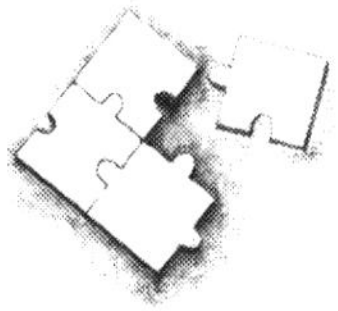

This **Professional Curiosity Self-Assessment Checklist** can be used individually or jointly and reflexively discussed. It is important to complete the column 'What helps me to achieve this?', which can form the basis of discussion taking place within the professional supervision relationship and set out the support needed to develop professional capability.

Professional Curiosity and Professional Context Checklist

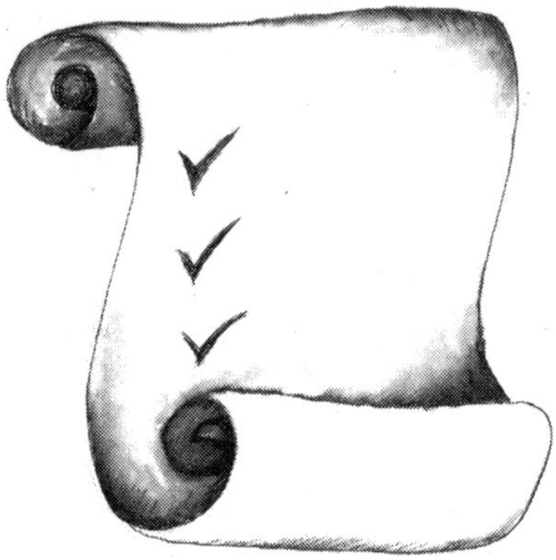

The third checklist below helps social work students and practice educators to identify and think about the role of organisational contexts in supporting or hampering the practice and development of professional curiosity. For a student with relatively less power than the practice educator, it may be difficult to name what could be different or how they would want the organisation or the supervision to improve. This could be the focus of a supervision relationship and will help to illuminate and connect to how practice cannot be fully understood without an appreciation of the organisational and wider social context. The questions should be used to explore how things are and what might be different.

Beliefs about my professional context	**Yes? No? Maybe?**	**Indicator**	**What can I do to improve the situation?**	**What gets in the way?**
I am supported by my practice educator/ supervisor/ manager and team.		• Discussions about practice concerns and dilemmas take place regularly. • I learn from discussions.		

Beliefs about my professional context	Yes? No? Maybe?	Indicator	What can I do to improve the situation?	What gets in the way?
The team or organisation where I am placed/work is stable and consistent.		• The team or organisation where I am placed/work is not going through a restructure or major change process.		
I am able to openly discuss fears and concerns about my work with my colleagues and practice educator/ supervisors/ managers.		• Communication is open in the team or organisation where I work. • People are not worried about being blamed when things go wrong. • The team is supportive.		
I get time to think and reflect.		• Workload is manageable.		
I get regular good-quality supervision.		• Supervision balances personal and professional development, and management of tasks and targets.		

→

Beliefs about my professional context	Yes? No? Maybe?	Indicator	What can I do to improve the situation?	What gets in the way?
I have good professional relationships with colleagues from other teams and disciplines.		• Sharing information with other professionals is open and works well.		
I keep good-quality contemporaneous records of contacts made with individuals and professionals.		• Records are written directly after contact with, or about, a child or adult. • Records are written in a way that acknowledges the person who they are about may read them.		

Translating this to a practice education scenario might involve checking with a student their value of the information as well as the degree of confidence, certainty and/or uncertainty of their knowledge or understanding and what might be missing. It also involves sharing the rationale that curiosity is enhanced or diminished under certain conditions.

Below is a personal anecdote which is shared to set out how establishing an open and trusting supervisory relationship creates the context for professional curiosity to flourish and highlights the responsibility of practice educators to be professionally curious about their own practice and genuinely seek open and honest feedback on their performance.

My final social work practice learning opportunity was split between two settings, a Child and Adolescent Mental Health Service (CAMHS) and a local authority child and family team. The supervision I received from my practice educator, a senior practitioner in the local authority team, I saw as inferior to the supervision in the CAMHS team from a family therapist social worker. The latter involved conversations that challenged my thinking and practice; I was encouraged to think about meta communication and ideas about family systems. The former was more managerial and service led, and on one occasion my practice educator admonished me for responding too quickly to a parent who had turned up at the office, saying it would give the wrong impression that everything could be dropped at a moment's notice. The practice educator also fell asleep during supervision and I was at a loss about what to do. The experience contributed to me expecting less from the local authority practice educator and the supervision. I shared this with the CAMHS practice educator and was encouraged to let the local authority practice educator know how I was feeling. I was also encouraged to see how the contexts, roles, duties and responsibilities were very different and would have had a bearing on how I perceived the two settings and practices.

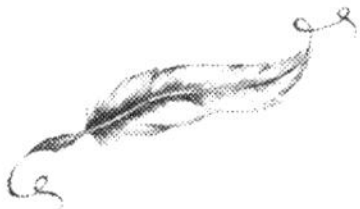

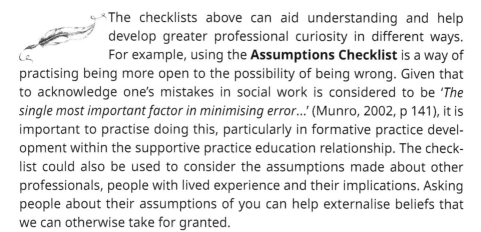

The checklists above can aid understanding and help develop greater professional curiosity in different ways. For example, using the **Assumptions Checklist** is a way of practising being more open to the possibility of being wrong. Given that to acknowledge one's mistakes in social work is considered to be '*The single most important factor in minimising error…*' (Munro, 2002, p 141), it is important to practise doing this, particularly in formative practice development within the supportive practice education relationship. The checklist could also be used to consider the assumptions made about other professionals, people with lived experience and their implications. Asking people about their assumptions of you can help externalise beliefs that we can otherwise take for granted.

The **Professional Curiosity Self-Assessment Checklist** and **Professional Curiosity and Professional Context Checklist** can be used in supervision and as a way of encouraging one's own critically curious mindset in relation to work with individuals and within intra- and inter-professional work.

Summary

There are many ways to interpret professional curiosity and its definition, applicability and usefulness for social work is emerging in the research literature. This chapter has sought to illustrate, further conceptualise and locate professional curiosity as part of modelling good practice and of teaching and supporting the integration of theory and skilful practice through the practice educator and student practitioner relationship. The checklists presented in this chapter are creative methods of putting into practice the type of critical professional curiosity that is considered to be a feature of safe effective practice.

Three key points

1. Developing professional curiosity has the potential to be transformative in terms of social workers' practice with people and its impact on people's lives. Thacker et al (2019) go so far as to say that professional curiosity has the potential to save lives.

2. Understanding what constitutes professional curiosity, including barriers and opportunities, is likely to improve practice. This includes understanding the significance of political, social and organisational contexts, interprofessional communication, and how risk is conceptualised and decisions are made. Theory and research let us know that we are constantly making assumptions and that because in making judgements we draw on fast thinking, our decisions are fallible to error and bias (Kahneman, 2012).

3. One of the main obstacles to achieving professional curiosity is managing the emotional dimension of social work; professional supervision is a key opportunity where awareness raising and processing of 'emotional labour' takes place. However, this presupposes that social work organisations have capacity and are set up in ways to invest in supervision, which is by no means standard. That said, practice education, defined by its one-to-one supervisory relationship (Dix, 2018), has a potentially transformative influence on future practice. Therefore, if professional curiosity could be developed at a pre-qualification learning stage of a social worker's practice orientation, this has the potential to make a significant difference to social workers' ability to practise as professional curiosity social workers, which could lead to greater practice efficacy.

References

Allnock, D and Miller, P (2013) *No One Noticed, No One Heard: A Study of Disclosures of Childhood Abuse*. London: National Society for the Prevention of Cruelty to Children.

Ball, P (2012) *Curiosity: How Science Became Interested in Everything.* Chicago, IL: University of Chicago Press.

Barton, A (2019) 'Practising Curiosity' Editorial. *Journal of Nursing Education*, 58(8): 439–40.

Brown, B (2010) The Power of Vulnerability. TED Talk. [online] Available at: https://blog.ted.com/being-vulnerable-about-vulnerability-qa-with-brene-brown (accessed 20 February 2022).

Burton, V and Revell, L (2017) Professional Curiosity in Child Protection: Thinking the Unthinkable in a Neo-Liberal World. *British Journal of Social Work*, 48(6): 1508–23.

Davies, L and Duckett, N (2016) *Proactive Child Protection and Social Work*. London: Sage/Learning Matters.

Dix, H (2018) Supervision Within Placement: What Students Can Expect and How to Get the Best From It. In Taplin, S (ed) *Innovations in Practice Learning* (pp 29–44). St Albans: Critical Publishing.

Einstein, A (1952) Letter to Carl Seelig, 11 March. *Einstein Archive*, 39-013.

Ferguson, H (2016) How Children Become Invisible in Child Protection Work: Findings from Research into Day-to-Day Social Work Practice. *The British Journal of Social Work*, 47(4): 1007–23.

Fook, J (2019) Critical Social Work and Social Justice. In Webb, S (ed) *The Routledge Handbook of Critical Social Work* (pp xxv–xxix). London: Routledge.

Freire, P (1970) *Pedagogy of the Oppressed.* London: Penguin Random House.

Healy, K (2000) *Social Work Practices*. London: Sage.

Kahneman, D (2012) *Thinking Fast and Slow.* London: Penguin Random House.

Kang, M, Krajbich, I M, Loewenstein, G, McClure, S M, Wang, J T and Camerer, C F (2009) The Wick in the Candle of Learning: Epistemic Curiosity Activates Reward Circuitry and Enhances Memory. *Psychological Science*, 20(8): 963–73.

Kidd, C and Hayden, B J (2015) The Psychology and Neuroscience of Curiosity. *Neuron Perspective*, 88(3): 449–60.

Laming, H (2003) *The Victoria Climbie Inquiry: Report of an Inquiry by Lord Laming*. [online] Available at: www.gov.uk/government/publications/the-victoria-climbie-inquiry-report-of-an-inquiry-by-lord-laming (accessed 20 February 2022).

Loewenstein, G (1994) The Psychology of Curiosity: A Review and Reinterpretation. *Psychology Bulletin*, 116(1): 75–98.

Mason, B (2017) Unpacking Safe Uncertainty. Online PowerPoint resource. [online] Available at: www.cfssw.org/sites/default/files/atoms/files/unpacking_safe_uncertainty_by_barry_mason.pdf (accessed 20 February 2022).

Mother Teresa of Calcutta (nd) Humility. [online] Available at: www.vaticansite.com/st-mother-teresa-quotes-humility (accessed 20 February 2022).

Munro, E (1999) Common Errors of Reasoning in Child Protection Work. *Child Abuse and Neglect*, 23(8): 745–58.

Munro, E (2002) *Effective Child Protection*. London: Sage.

Price Williams, D and Chisholm, T (2018) Reflections on a Serious Case Review: How Health Recommendations Have Changed Since 2011 and the Impact of Professional Curiosity on Health Assessments. *Adoption & Fostering*, 42(2): 201–5.

Thacker, H, Anka, A and Penhale, B (2019) Could Curiosity Save Lives? An Exploration into the Value of Employing Professional Curiosity and Partnership Work in Safeguarding Adults Under The Care Act 2014. *The Journal of Adult Protection*, 21(5): 252–67.

Webb, S (ed) (2019) *The Routledge Handbook of Critical Social Work*. London: Routledge.

It's not my fault

Demi Bowler

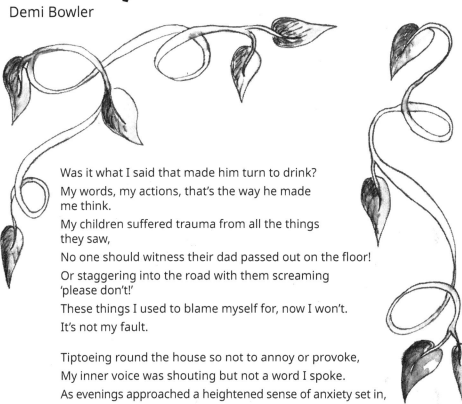

Was it what I said that made him turn to drink?
My words, my actions, that's the way he made me think.
My children suffered trauma from all the things they saw,
No one should witness their dad passed out on the floor!
Or staggering into the road with them screaming 'please don't!'
These things I used to blame myself for, now I won't.
It's not my fault.

Tiptoeing round the house so not to annoy or provoke,
My inner voice was shouting but not a word I spoke.
As evenings approached a heightened sense of anxiety set in,
Tonight would be the norm soon the verbal abuse would begin.
Shutting the bedroom door so to protect youthful ears,
Trying hard to disguise my face blotchy and stained with tears.
Remember... It's not my fault.

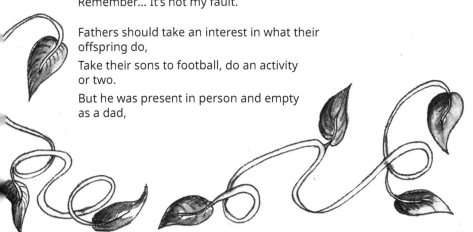

Fathers should take an interest in what their offspring do,
Take their sons to football, do an activity or two.
But he was present in person and empty as a dad,

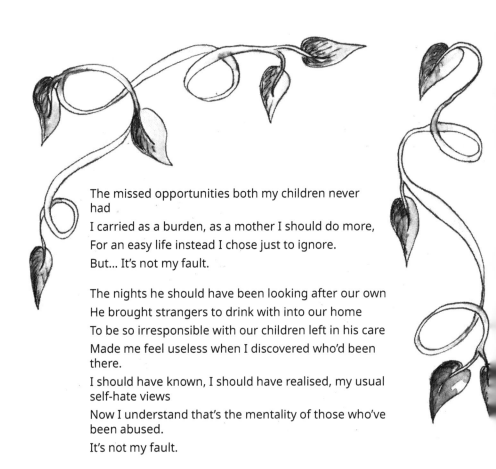

The missed opportunities both my children never had
I carried as a burden, as a mother I should do more,
For an easy life instead I chose just to ignore.
But... It's not my fault.

The nights he should have been looking after our own
He brought strangers to drink with into our home
To be so irresponsible with our children left in his care
Made me feel useless when I discovered who'd been there.
I should have known, I should have realised, my usual self-hate views
Now I understand that's the mentality of those who've been abused.
It's not my fault.

Moving forward with my life of which he no longer is a part,
I'm working on myself and mending my broken heart.
Focusing on my children, they'll be happier now he's gone,
Reiterating to them it's nothing they've done wrong.
The fault lies with one person who'll never think he's to blame,
Lies, deceitfulness, alcohol and no morals were his shame,
Not mine... It's not my fault.

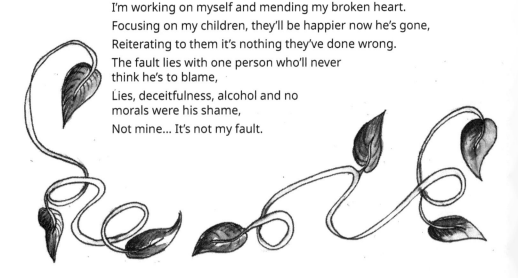

Chapter 8

Getting creative with endings

Claire Skilleter

And so we begin...

We all have experience of endings in our personal and work lives, some planned, some unexpected, some helpful and some painful. In fact, in our professional role we experience endings daily, be that the end of a telephone call, the end of a working relationship, the end of a home visit, or the end of a supervision session. By the nature of being time limited, every practice learning opportunity has an enforced ending imposed onto the student, the individuals they are working with and the practice educator. Rosenthal Gelman et al (2007) note there is little written about how to support students and supervisors to manage this enforced ending in the most effective way possible. Indeed, the pressure of finishing or transferring the students' work with individuals, producing the final report and completing the portfolio paperwork can overshadow the importance of taking time to prepare for and mark the end of the practice learning opportunity. Often, the significance of endings is underestimated, yet getting the ending right can often either enrich what has come before or take away from any progress made within the student–practice educator relationship.

In this chapter, four practice tools for endings will be provided. Congruent with the four-stage model of relationship building (McColgan and McMullin, 2017) referred to in Chapter 1, we need to pay as much attention to the ending of a relationship as to the previous stages because it can provide an opportunity to reinforce an authentic and empathic relationship. However, conversations about endings can be challenging and, as mentioned above, a badly managed ending can sabotage work that has taken place previously (Wilson et al, 2008). The practice tools in this chapter act in line with Winnicott's 'third thing' or 'third object' (Community Care, 2010) in that they provide both student and practice educator with something else to focus on while this difficult issue is being discussed, potentially making these conversations a little easier.

Endings Sensory Stick Person

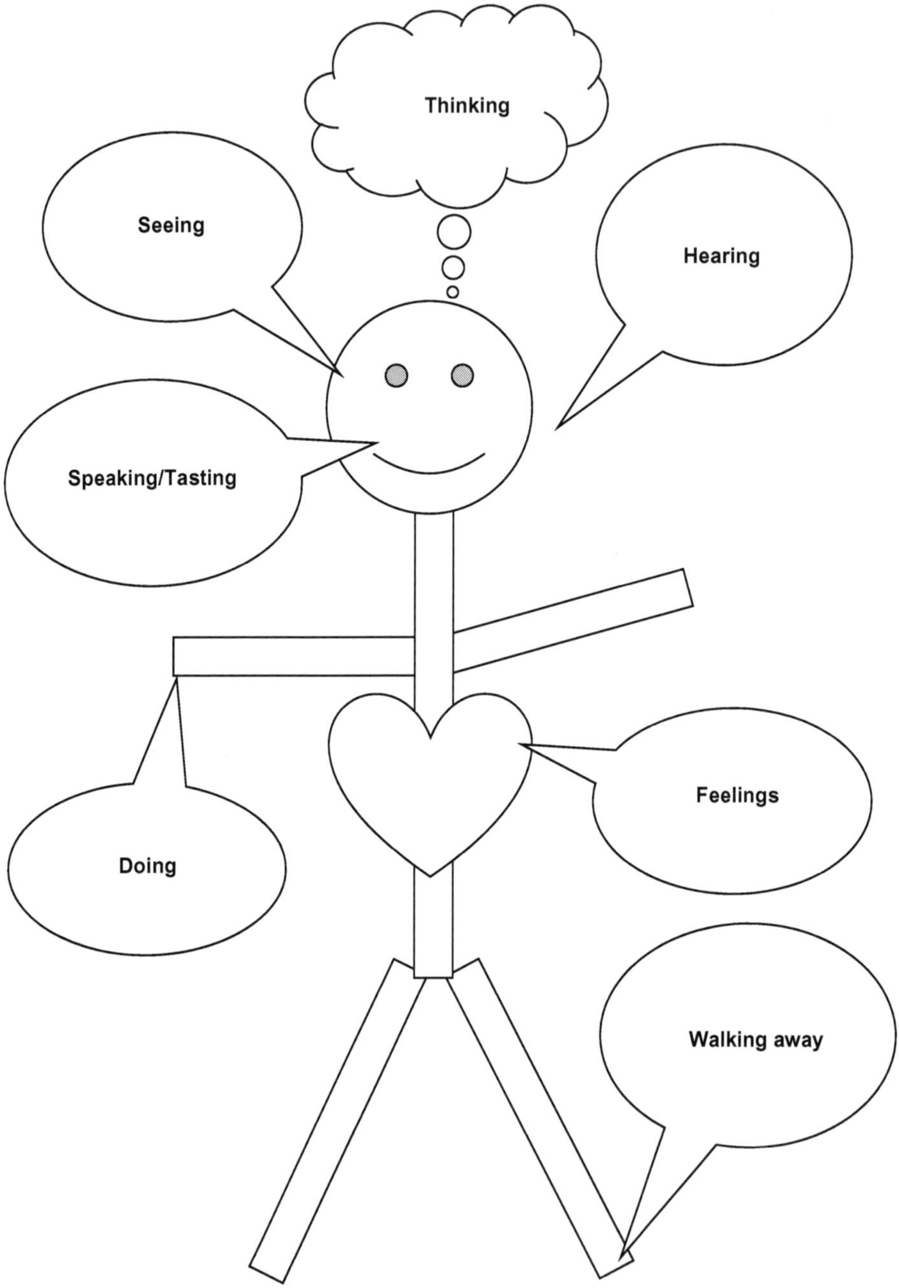

'I've learned that people will forget what you said, people will forget what you did, but people will never forget how you made them feel.'

This famous Maya Angelou quote resonates with me and embodies this chapter well. I am really interested in the use of senses in social work. Maybe this stems from working with children who have experienced trauma and thinking about how trauma is experienced through the senses (Treisman, 2017). My original stick person was devised to aid my work with children when exploring likes and dislikes. I then developed the tool to help prepare children for endings and have since expanded it to use with students. Historically, I often found that when working with students my conversations around preparing to end typically involved tasks focused on closure paperwork, work with families, report deadlines, ensuring goodbye visits with individuals and planning the student's 'leaving do'. I reflected that these conversations were usually led by me with little input from the student. They also seemed to miss the vital component of what endings might mean for the student and how the student may be experiencing the ending process. In addition, my conversations were not modelling practice that the student could necessarily use in their work with people with lived experience. From this, I developed the ***Endings Sensory Stick Person*** *as a way of talking about and planning for the end of the practice learning opportunity to provide the student with some power and control over the ending, modelling more meaningful conversations about ending that can be transferred to work with people.*

Let's talk about feelings

Firstly, it is important not to make assumptions about the student's previous experiences of endings, or how the student may wish to mark the end of their practice learning opportunity. Equally, it is important to support the student to think about how to end well with individuals. This is a useful tool to undertake around the mid-point in the practice learning opportunity. The **Endings Sensory Stick Person** allows the student to explore thoughts and feelings about the end of the practice learning opportunity, and choose how to prepare for the end and how to mark it. This in turns promotes discussion about how the student will manage their endings with individuals. The **Endings Sensory Stick Person** should be revisited at regular intervals between the midway point and the end of the practice learning opportunity. This allows time for different reflections on the planned ending and for new ideas and thoughts to be added as they emerge.

The stick person's roots

Social work as a multisensorial experience is gaining more attention in social work literature. For example, Ferguson's (2016) work about child protection social work and home visiting pays attention to the sensory elements of visiting families, such as smell. He notes how sensory elements of family environments can trigger emotional responses in social workers, such as experiencing anxiety or feeling frozen. The **Endings Sensory Stick Person** activity is a sensory and visual approach influenced by the work of Morriss (2017) on sensory ethnography, and Clark and Morriss' (2015) work around visual approaches. Morriss (2017) explains that sensory ethnography in relation to research closely attends to the senses throughout the research process. In addition, Clark and Morriss (2015) suggest that visual approaches can be powerful because they provide a way of sensing, experiencing, expressing and seeing the social work world. By using the **Endings Sensory Stick Person**, it is hoped that students and practice educators can pay attention to planning endings in a sensorial way and think about how endings may trigger thoughts and feelings.

The how to...

When working virtually, the **Endings Sensory Stick Person** template can be shared online and completed electronically. When working in person, the student can draw themselves as a stick person on a large sheet of paper, decorate as they wish, and the discussion is recorded in speech bubbles around the drawing.

For each speech bubble the practice educator guides the conversation.

Thinking (head) – This is a sensitive area of discussion and needs to be managed with care. It can be offered as an opportunity for the student to think about how their own experiences of endings may influence their reactions to professional endings. Questions that could be useful are:

- what memories or thoughts do you have about previous endings?
- how might those memories or thoughts influence this ending?

Recently I used the ***Endings Sensory Stick Person*** *with Jeanette, a social work student in her first-level practice learning opportunity. When I asked her the questions from the 'thinking (head)' section of this tool, she began the conversation certain that her own experiences had not influenced her reactions to endings. As Jeanette and I talked about this further and I probed deeper, she became aware that her strong feelings about providing an explanation to individuals about why work was ending was influenced by personal endings she had experienced where explanations had not been given to her. This helped Jeanette to understand that indeed her own experiences of endings had influenced her beliefs about endings and how they should be managed with people with lived experience.*

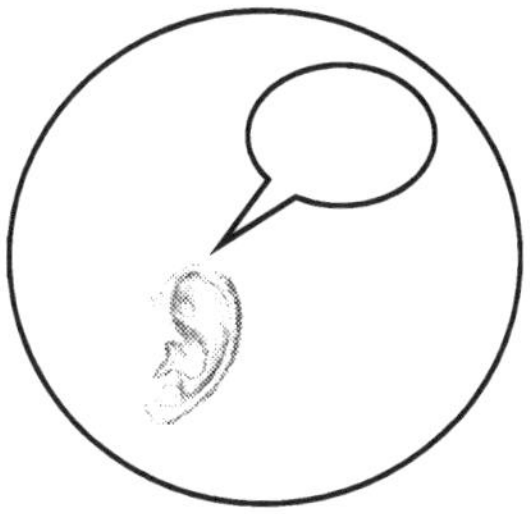

Hearing (ears) – This provides an opportunity for the student to think about what they would like to hear about at the end of their practice learning opportunity and from whom. Useful questions could be:

- what would you like to hear about when we end our work?
- who would you like to hear from?
- why might it be important to hear from that person?

There is opportunity here to think about gathering feedback from colleagues and people with lived experience, and how this might be achieved.

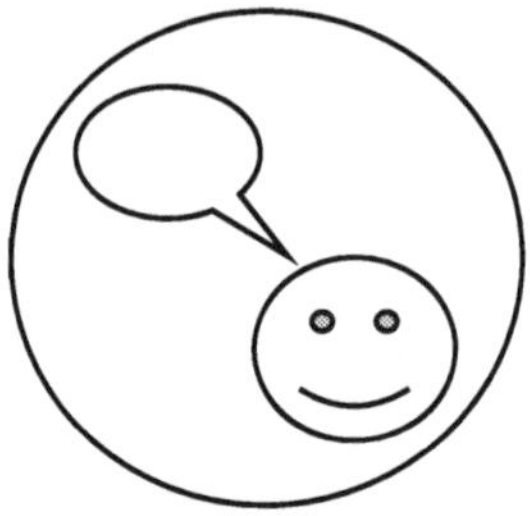

Seeing (eyes) – This is an opportunity to visualise the end or the final day of the practice learning opportunity. The practice educator might ask questions such as:

- what would you like your ending to look like?
- who would you like to see on your final day? And why?

Speaking and tasting (mouth) – This is an opportunity to think about who the student may wish to speak with at the end of the practice learning opportunity and how this will be achieved. Useful questions might be:

- what might you like to say when we end our work?
- who will you need to speak to?
- how will we ensure there is an opportunity to do that?

In addition, asking questions such as 'What food would you like to eat on your final day?' and 'What celebratory meal might you like?' provides a light-hearted way to consider any special nurturing food or celebratory events the student may want to mark the end of the practice learning opportunity. When a practice educator colleague of mine used these questions with a student, it resulted in the student and practice educator discovering a shared love of cheese, which then led to a team wine and cheese evening to mark the end of the practice learning opportunity. You never know where this question could take you...!

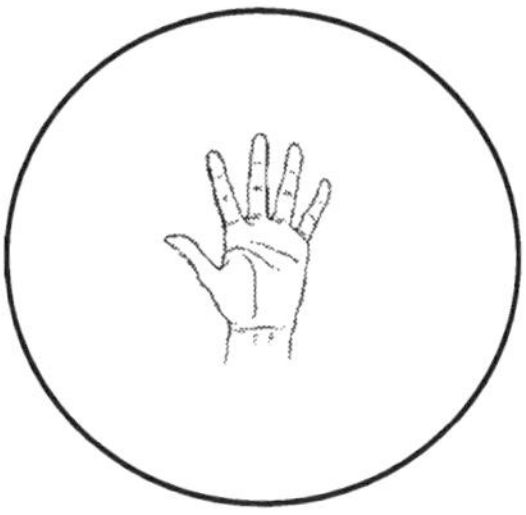

Doing (hands) – This section provides an opportunity to discuss what the student might like to do with the team, practice educator or people with lived experience to mark the end of their practice learning opportunity. It might also include how the student will start preparing individuals for the end of their working relationship. Useful questions may be:

- what do we need to do before our ending?
- what would you like to do on your final day/week to mark your ending?
- how will you involve each person in planning for the end of your work together?

Feelings (heart) – In this section the practice educator and student discuss feelings associated with the end of the practice learning opportunity. Discussions from the 'thinking' section of the activity may be interwoven with this part of the activity. Questions that could be helpful are:

- what do you feel right now about ending the practice learning opportunity?
- what might you feel as you near the final day?
- why might you feel that way?
- how might you manage those feelings?
- who might support you with that?
- how might you express those feelings?

Revisiting the **Endings Sensory Stick Person** at regular intervals as the practice learning opportunity approaches an end will provide an opportunity to reflect on how feelings may change and the possible reasoning behind this. There is an important focus here on emotional containment and how feelings will be managed. As Bion (1962) suggests, emotional containment is accepting and taking in an individual's feelings and emotions and returning them to them in a manageable form, thus helping the individual think straight. Thinking about emotional containment in four elements may be helpful, as seen below.

Acceptance of feelings = *Accept the way the student feels*
Naming of feelings = *Help the student find the words to name the feelings*
Understand the feelings = *Help the student to understand where the feelings come from and why*
Management of feelings = *Support the student to think of ways to manage the feelings*

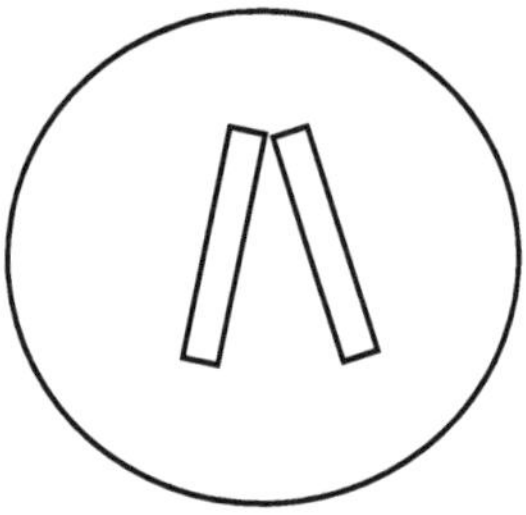

Walking away (feet) – This section of the discussion focuses on how to ensure the student will walk away from the practice learning opportunity with what they need for the future. This area of the discussion is also helpful for planning any outstanding learning needs for the second part of the practice learning opportunity. Revisiting the **Endings Sensory Stick Person** at future supervisions will help to review these. Helpful questions could include:

- what new learning do you want to achieve before you walk away?
- how might you do that?
- how will you know this has happened?
- imagining moving on from this practice learning opportunity, what will you carry with you in your toolkit?
- what might make it hard to walk away?
- what would make it easier?

And in our day-to-day practice

The activity can be used in the same way with individuals with some adjustment to the language. For example, 'final visit' instead of 'final day'. The activity can be particularly helpful to complete with children, especially those who have experienced a lack of control over previous endings in their lives.

End of Placement Reflection Letter

Dear future self,

As I end this student practice learning opportunity and move forward with the next chapter of my social work career, I want to remember:

Experiences

What were my most positive experiences?

Why were they positive?

How have they impacted on me?

Feelings

What feelings have I experienced during this practice learning opportunity?

Why did I feel this way?

How did I manage these feelings?

Values and beliefs

What values and beliefs have been important to me?

Why were they important?

How will I hold onto these?

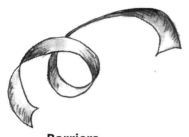

Barriers

What barriers did I face? What were these related to?

Why did these barriers arise?

How did I manage these barriers or overcome them?

Learning

What is my biggest learning?

Why is this my biggest learning?

How has it influenced my practice?

Skills and tools

What new skills and tools have I developed?

Why are they useful?

How will I take these forward?

My best advice from this practice learning opportunity experience:

Letter writing holds fond memories for me, as a child and young person (when there were no mobile phones and my parents couldn't afford a landline phone until I was in my late teens). I used to write letters to my cousin in Canada and to my best friend who moved away when we were both 10 years old. I recall the freedom of writing my feelings and thoughts on specially purchased stationery and the memory of waiting excitedly, a week or so later, for the post to arrive. I kept the letters I received in a precious box and would return to them when I needed to feel some comfort or connection with these special people. Later, when working in a family therapy team, my colleagues and I used letter writing with citizens as a way of reflecting on their session, noting achievements or 'wondering' about aspects of what had been shared in the session. I guess it was a natural progression that when working with students, I thought about letter writing as a way of reflecting on their practice learning experience; it seemed to me that this might be a meaningful way to focus reflections, but also to create a tool that could provide comfort, motivation and connection when revisited at a later date.

Dear myself

An **End of Placement Reflection Letter** is a letter to yourself from yourself for both the practice educator and the student to complete. It aims to support both to reflect, review and consolidate the knowledge gained from the practice learning opportunities. For the practice educator it is also a method for recording learning for continuing professional development (CPD). Practice educators could upload their letter onto the Social Work England website as an example of their CPD. The student could add their letter into their practice portfolio or use the letter template as a creative way for writing a final reflective piece.

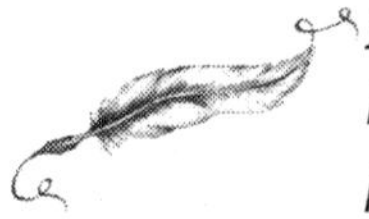

I usually complete my own practice educator ***End of Placement Reflection Letter*** *alongside the student. I think this helps to promote the message that we are always learning as a lifelong process. Sharing our letters in our final student supervision feels reciprocal, in that we are exchanging and appreciating our learning, which the other individual has contributed to. In turn this helps to address the power imbalance, as*

it promotes the message that we have both been learners. I now have several ***End of Placement Reflection Letters*** *stored in my box. When read in chronological order they provide a really interesting account of my practice educator journey. They are also useful when I need reassurance about my own abilities or when I need inspiration or ideas for managing a particular issue with a current student.*

Origins

Letter writing is closely associated with narrative therapy (White and Epston, 1990) and is often used in therapeutic work (Treisman, 2017). In the context of reflective practice (Schön,1983), the **End of Placement Reflection Letter** enables reflection 'on action'. The letter also uses the *What? Why? How?* question framework (Maclean, 2016), thus promoting critical reflection. Maclean explains that the 'why' question is particularly important for professional practice as it provides the analysis of a situation. As both student and practice educator complete the activity and share it with each other, it attempts to address the power imbalance and end the practice learning opportunity reflection in a reciprocal manner.

How to weave this into the fabric of the practice learning opportunity

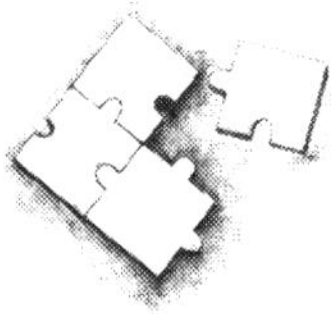

In the final weeks of the practice learning opportunity, the student and the practice educator individually complete their **End of Placement Reflection Letter**. The letters are shared and discussed at one of the final supervision sessions, which promotes further reflection. At each heading the practice educator and student write or draw their thoughts and answer the questions posed by the letter. The headings in the letter can be adapted or other headings could be used. This practice tool is easily adapted to virtual working as the letter template can be completed and shared online. Alternatively, the student and practice educator may choose to complete the letter as a large collage or drawing, which could be physically shown via video link, or use websites such as Microsoft Teams or canva.com where both can jointly contribute towards its creation.

Dear citizen

The concept of an 'end of work letter' can be used with people with lived experience as a method to process and mark the ending of a piece of work with a practitioner. The basic premise is to support individuals to look back, review and consolidate learning from their work with the practitioner, but also to look forwards. The letter can be offered as an activity to undertake with the practitioner as work is nearing a close. We know that endings can be hard and for some individuals the letter may be too difficult to write, and so choice, time and support are important. The end of work letter can provide a meaningful way to review the work undertaken and act as a tool to refer back to when the individual may need comfort, motivation or helpful reminders. An end of work letter can be used to encourage further change and promote the idea that the person can use tools and learning from your work together into the future.

The headings and words can be changed to suit the individual and the circumstances, but you could use this as something to start from.

Helpful things to do – During our work together, what activities have you learnt which are helpful to do when things feel tricky? Why do you think that helps you? Where are your helpful places to go? Why do you find those places helpful? What things have helped you most in the past?

Helpful people to call (or email/text) – Who are your helpful people to speak to? What makes that person a good person to call? Are there any organisations that may be able to help in the future?

Reminders of learning – What have you learnt about yourself or others during our work together? What are the main points you would want to remember from our work together?

Great things about me – What positive qualities have you noticed about yourself during our work together? What great things have other people noticed about you?

A memory that helps me realise I can manage – Can you think of a time during our work together when you overcame a difficult situation? What skills, strategies or qualities enabled you to overcome this? What did you learn from that?

Hopes for the future – What are your hopes or goals for the future? What might you need to do to get there?

When I use an end of work letter, it is very much a supported and joint enterprise. The individual and I write the letter as we have the conversation, prompted by the headings above. I ask whether the person would like to write, or whether I should write. I ask whether they would like me to type up the letter afterwards. I try to make the letter as special as possible, signifying the value I place on that person, so depending on the individual's preferences I may put the letter in a special envelope or roll it up and tie it with a ribbon. I then leave the letter with the person on our final meeting. Many years ago, I used this activity with a group of women who were survivors of domestic abuse. About five years later, I bumped into one of the women while shopping. The first thing she said to me was 'I still look at my letter, to remind myself how strong I actually am'. This was one of those golden social work moments, which I will always remember.

Placement Memory Jar

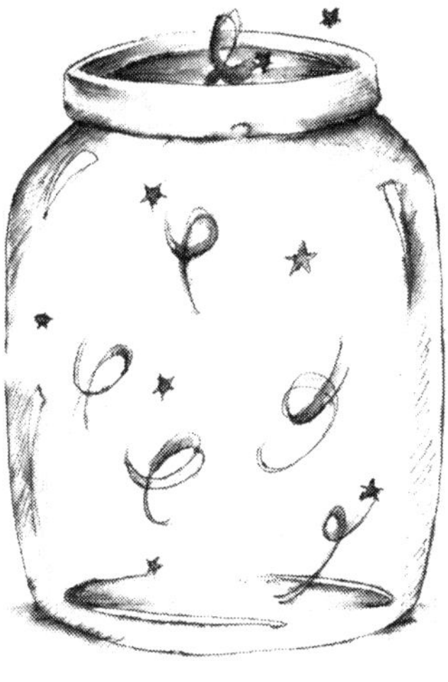

I have known about and used loss and bereavement jars with children for many years. I was always struck with the depth of conversation that ensued from making the jar and, once made, the importance of the jar to the child. I am always thinking about experiential learning for students (Kolb, 1984), particularly in my role where I often work with groups of students. I wanted to teach students about loss and bereavement jars but was also aware that group work exploring loss and bereavement in such a personal way was not appropriate or safe. I therefore decided to teach the students about the tool via reflecting on the loss of something different and more manageable – their practice learning experience.

Memories in a jar

This activity is an adaptation of loss and bereavement jars, which are often used by organisations supporting children and families with bereavement. The child or adult creates a jar of different coloured layers of sand or salt, each layer representing a different memory or characteristic of the bereaved relative. In the context of preparing for the end of the practice learning opportunity, the loss and bereavement jar is adapted to a make a **Placement Memory Jar**, with each layer of coloured salt representing a memory, stage or feeling the student has experienced whie completing the practice learning opportunity. As with the **End of Placement Reflection Letter**, the practice educator could also make their own **Placement Memory Jar**. The activity should be undertaken as the practice learning opportunity ends. The materials (see below) can be provided by the practice educator and the activity undertaken in an in-person supervision. For virtual working this activity is more challenging. However, given enough notice the student can be encouraged to collect a jar, salt and chalk as they are all inexpensive items and the activity could be undertaken in a virtual supervision.

Compared to the **End of Placement Reflection Letter**, the **Placement Memory Jar** is a physical activity with lots of spoken reflection and minimal written recording. The activity is ideal for students who want to experience a more active way of reflecting by using creative practical arts. However, there are some sensory issues to check out when using this practice tool. For example, some individuals are not comfortable with the texture of salt or chalk or the noise of rubbing the chalk into the salt.

Philosophy

The **Placement Memory Jar** recognises the importance of creative arts in social work. It is known that using creative arts and techniques is beneficial for promoting creativity in practice as well as reflection (Maclean et al, 2018). The **Placement Memory Jar** is drawn from the philosophy of loss and bereavement jars, which are a well-known therapeutic technique used by many counsellors and organisations. The process of making a jar supports bereaved relatives to explore usually positive, happy memories of their deceased relative and creating a jar is, in part, to remember them.

DIY

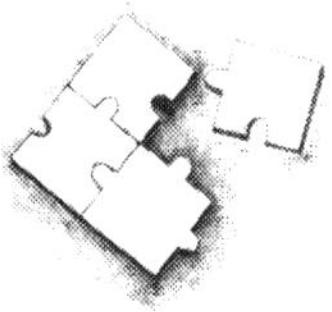

Materials needed:

- a range of small clean spice/mini jam jars;
- table salt;
- coloured chalk sticks;
- sticky tape;
- A4 paper;
- table cover.

Invite the student to choose a jar. This could be a jar they like or one with personal significance to them. For example, a curry powder jar because they have lived off takeaways during the practice learning experience, or a tall jar because they have grown in their learning between practice learning opportunities. The student chooses approximately the correct amount of table salt to fill the jar. They spend some time thinking about five memories from the practice learning opportunity. These could be five stages they have identified over the practice learning opportunity, five feelings, five significant pieces of work, five pieces of learning, a mixture of all of these or something else. The student then divides the salt into five separate amounts and each is placed on a separate piece of A4 paper. These will form the five layers to represent the identified memories. Some memories might be more significant than others and this can be reflected in the size of the layer (so more salt for the more significant memories).

Each layer of salt should be a different colour; the student should reflect on which colour is most appropriate. For example, the student may associate a certain colour with a feeling, piece of work or learning. Taking one of the five amounts of salt and holding the chosen coloured chalk stick in a vertical position, the chalk stick is rubbed over the salt to colour it. Glitter could also be added if desired. The longer the chalk is rubbed over the salt, the deeper the shade of the colour. When the layer of salt is coloured, the student lifts the A4 paper with the coloured salt on it and, holding it rather like a funnel, pours it into the jar. Knock the jar gently on the table to help the salt to settle. This is repeated for the five layers.

As with all the practice tools, the conversation with the student while they are making the **Placement Memory Jar** or after the jar is completed is vital to gain the most reflection and learning from the activity. Exploring each memory by using curious questioning will help to draw out the student's reflective thinking and can support the development of emotional intelligence. Depending on the memories or feelings being discussed, the practice educator may use a variety of different questioning and discussion techniques to enable the student to reflect further as they create their jar. Questions which focus on emotions and self-awareness can be very useful. Again, using a what, why and how framework may be helpful. For example, some of the following questions could be useful.

- What did you feel?
- What impact did that have?
- What might the impact of that be moving forward?
- Why do you think you felt like that?
- Why was that a positive moment for you?
- Why do you think your feelings changed?
- Why do you think you responded in that way?
- How might you manage those feelings?
- How might those feelings impact on you using the activity with people with lived experience?
- How do you feel about that now?
- How did you know that?

When the jar is completed, the lid of the jar is replaced and strengthened by adding clear sticky tape around it. The student then makes a decorative note to accompany the jar, listing the meaning of each layer.

I have now used this activity with several student groups. I am constantly asking friends and relatives to save me their spice jars and searching for reduced-priced jumbo chalk! When I use the activity with my student groups, I am always struck by the level of reflective conversation that is created as they make the jars and the pride with which students take their jars home, talking about where they will keep them as reminders of their practice learning journey.

A life in jars

In the context of students ending practice learning opportunities, the activity is transferrable for the student to use with individuals to mark the end of their working relationship. It can provide an opportunity for student and individuals to reflect on their work together. Each layer could be linked to the stages of the work they have completed, the individuals' memories or feelings about the work, or simply things that the person wants to remember about the student.

Appreciative Present Posters

Many years ago, I facilitated several women's self-esteem building groups where I first devised this activity as an ending exercise for the women in the group. As each group ended the women would contribute to appreciative present posters for each other. It was a method to show appreciation for each other and to provide a gift of kindness at the end of their work together.

A present

An **Appreciative Present Poster** is a gift for the student to mark the end of the practice learning opportunity and is created by the practice educator and their team for the student. Contributions to the **Appreciative Present Poster** could be quoted in the student's final report.

The science behind the poster

Appreciative Present Posters are aligned to a strengths-based perspective (Saleebey, 2012) and fit well with providing specific feedback to students. In the spirit of appreciation, the activity is linked to appreciative inquiry and the act of valuing and noticing the best in others.

Let's get down to it...

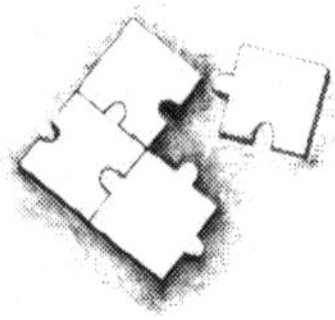

A large sheet of paper is required, and a present box with ribbon and gift tag is drawn onto the paper for the student. Each person who is saying 'goodbye' to the student writes a personal message on the present. This should be specific to the student and describe something positive they have appreciated or noticed about them. For example, 'I liked the way you always said hello in the mornings' or 'I noticed when you worked with H, you always gave him time to talk'. When complete, the **Appreciative Present Poster** can be given to the student in a number of ways, depending on what is appropriate. However, making the poster feel special, like a present, is important. Like an end of work letter, it could be rolled up, tied with a ribbon and presented at a leaving event or sent in the mail as a surprise. For virtual working, appreciative comments could be collected from team members online and inserted into a Word document version of the present or a PowerPoint presentation with meaningful music added.

*Having used the **Appreciative Present Poster** many times now with students and groups, I can still be surprised about how much the posters can mean to individuals. I have seen many a teary eye as people look at the poster they have received. I think that the act of seeing and reading what others have noticed, appreciated and*

clearly described in terms of positive character traits, practices or behaviours can be really meaningful and emotive. As I was writing this chapter, I was struck by how with recent pressures of work and the isolation of working at home during a pandemic I had not appreciated two of my closest colleagues enough. This prompted me to write an appreciative email to them and I resolved to try to keep the thinking behind the ***Appreciative Present Poster*** *more at the forefront of my mind.*

Posters and people

Appreciative Present Posters are easily adapted to endings with people with lived experience. The practitioner creates an **Appreciative Present Poster** for the individual as an ending gift. This could include comments solely from the practitioner and can include comments from other professionals working as part of a multidisciplinary group. The activity is very transferrable to group work.

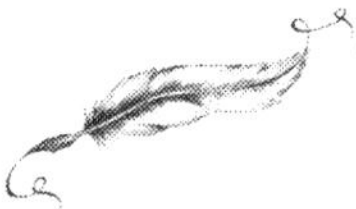

I use this activity with groups of students who have worked together over the course of their practice learning opportunity in 'student hubs'. At the final session all the students contribute to each other's ***Appreciative Present Poster*** *with specific positive comments about what they have appreciated about their student colleagues over the course of the practice learning opportunity.*

Endings

Providing a meaningful ending can allow the opportunity for students to manage what it feels like to leave and leave others behind. It also provides an opportunity to experience what a thoughtful ending can feel like, thus modelling the practice we want our students to take forward into their work with individuals for years to come. Endings are an emotive subject; many of us may be triggered into thoughts and feelings related to previous loss and grief as a result of talking about endings in the present. Whichever tool a practice educator and student use, you, as the practice educator, are the best tool. Any practice tool, when used in the context of a trusting, reciprocal and emotionally containing supervisory relationship, will feel safer and more meaningful.

Three key points

1. Many of the tools described in this chapter may make students feel exposed and vulnerable. Importantly, it will be vital to help the student to feel safe and secure while using the tools. As described in Chapter 1, spending time from the beginning of the practice learning opportunity creating a safe base from which the student can explore their own reactions, thoughts and feelings is vitally important for students to gain the most from these exercises.

2. As practice educators we are assessing students and have considerable power. This power may impact the student feeling unable to be entirely honest within some of these activities. It will be important to acknowledge and discuss this power throughout the practice learning opportunity. Chapter 1, 'Let's start at the beginning', describes how conversations around this can begin at the 'supervision chair' stage but should remain on the agenda throughout the learning experience. At the beginning of any of the activities described in this chapter, one might ask of both yourself and the student 'what might the impact of power be as we undertake this activity?' and 'how might we manage that?'

3. The practice educator promoting and understanding the potential benefits and challenges of using the tools is important in terms of social work practice and the development of self-awareness. Endings can be an emotive area for any of us. Experiencing the activities in this chapter with a trusted colleague before using them with students might be helpful in terms of your own experiential learning and developing self-awareness around your own triggers and emotions in relation to endings.

References

Bion, W (1962) *Learning from Experience.* London: Heinemann.

Clark, A and Morriss, L (2015) The Use of Visual Methodologies in Social Work Research Over the Last Decade: A Narrative Review and Some Questions for the Future. *Qualitative Social Work*, 16(1): 29–43.

Community Care (2010) Play and Creative Arts Help Children in Care Explore Their Lives. [online] Available at: www.communitycare.co.uk/2010/04/22/play-and-creative-arts-help-children-in-care-explore-their-lives (accessed 22 February 2022).

Ferguson, H (2016) How Children Become Invisible in Child Protection Work: Findings from Research into Day-to-day Social Work Practice. *British Journal of Social Work*, 47(4): 1007–23.

Kolb, D (1984) *Experiential Learning: Experience as the Source of Learning and Development*. Englewood Cliffs, NJ: Prentice Hall.

Maclean, S (2016) *Reflective Practice Cards.* Lichfield, Staffordshire: Kirwin Maclean Associates Ltd.

Maclean, S, Finch, J and Tedam, P (2018) *SHARE: A New Model for Social Work.* Lichfield: Kirwin Maclean Associates Ltd.

McColgan, M and McMullin, C (2017) *Doing Relationship-based Social Work: A Practical Guide to Building Relationships and Enabling Change.* London: Jessica Kingsley Publishers.

Morriss, L (2017) Multisensoriality and Social Work Research. *Qualitative Social Work*, 16(3): 291–9.

Rosenthal Gelman, C, Fernandez, P, Hausman, N, Miller, S and Weiner, M (2007) Challenging Endings: First Year Interns' Experiences with Premature Termination and Discussion Points for Supervisory Guidance. *Clinical Social Work Journal*, 35(2): 79–90.

Saleebey, D (2012) *The Strengths Perspective in Social Work Practice: International Edition*. New York: Pearson.

Schön, D (1983) *The Reflective Practitioner*. San Francisco: Jossey Bass.

Treisman, K (2017) *A Therapeutic Treasure Box for Working with Children and Adolescents with Developmental Trauma: Creative Techniques and Activities.* London: Jessica Kingsley Press.

White, M and Epston, D (1990) *Narrative Means to Therapeutic Ends.* New York: W W Norton and Company.

Wilson, K, Ruch, G, Lymbery, M and Cooper, A (2008) *Social Work: An Introduction to Contemporary Practice.* London: Pearson Education.

Since you left

Makayla Bowler

You don't call me half as often,
you always arrive late,
and somehow it's just those little things
that put me in a state.

I know that moving forward isn't easy
and you say you try your best,
but I just don't know how to feel,
since you left.

Every single time you see me
you say how much I've grown,
but I haven't gained or lost an inch
for at least a few years
that's all I know.

And I wish that you could put my heart at ease,
and put my mind to rest.
But I only feel the distance,
since you left.

And you tell me to move on,
move forward,
to simply just get over it,
When I still don't know how to feel
since you left.

You say that you care about me,
but those are words.
Where is the action to show
that you still want me around,
when deep down I know you are letting go?

Maybe I'm just asking for too much
because you never chose me
and I have to digest
this feeling of neglect,
that's been exposed
since you left.

Summary

Firstly, we would like to thank you. As practice educators, you are the unsung heroes of social work education. You are instrumental in developing the future generations of social workers. This often includes being the 'architects of learning'. What this means is that you equip and enable students to build knowledge, develop skills and thrive in social work, from within a learning partnership (Beverley and Worsley, 2007). As you may already know, there is no one 'perfect' way of learning, as people possess different abilities, networks and preferences of what and how to learn. We believe that creativity can transcend old patterns of thinking into something more meaningful, where curiosity, credibility, confidence and critical thinking are the driving forces within practice education. Through this book, we have created a space for creativity to hold value for the individual practice educator and student, and beyond. It is where connections in relationships may be strengthened, with the hope that it will contribute towards a culture of creative learning. As such, the tools have been designed with differences in context and purpose in mind, so you will find something that works for you, your practice and your creative potential, whatever the situation.

One of the key messages within this book is that creativity emerges in and through practice. Put simply, what we mean by 'practice' is:

1. the practice of learning;
2. social work practice;
3. practice education;
4. the practice within the student–practice educator relationship;
5. the practice of 'doing' creativity.

This suggests that, as practice educators, creativity is embedded within the fabric of what you do. However, we want to reassure you that you do not necessarily have to possess creative capabilities to enhance a student's learning and experience while undertaking a practice learning opportunity. Creativity is not just for the few practitioners who are good at drawing or doing role-play, who have those great, original ideas or who are known as the 'creative type'. **Creativity is for everyone and it can be cultivated with practice.** We recognise that there are different pressures that practice educators face, which can impact your creative courage, such as time, energy, workload and attending to multiple responsibilities. Yet, fostering a creative learning space may simply be about drawing on the different tools in this book and using them with a student in supervision.

So, now it is for you to take the next steps. This book allows you to consider your creative ability, interest and practical application of creativity within the practice learning experience and we hope you incorporate some of these ideas within your 'toolkit' to boost your creative mindset and practice.

Reference

Beverley, A and Worsley, A (2007) *Learning & Teaching in Social Work Practice*. London: Palgrave Macmillan.

Appendix 1

Tool: The Supervision Chair

There are six stages to building **The Supervision Chair**; the practice educator and the student talk though each stage and record the discussions, on either the template, large drawing, model or collage.

1. Chair legs – What do you need in order to feel that supervision and your supervisor are available, stable and predictable?
2. Chair seat – What do we need to know about each other so that we can sit comfortably with each other? How can we learn more about each other? How do our values, beliefs, life and work experiences, cultural similarities and differences impact on how we 'sit' with each other? What do we need to acknowledge in terms of the seat of power and privilege? How will we sit with and manage challenge or conflict?
3. Chair arms – What do you need from me as a practice educator to feel accepted, emotionally contained and supported? How will you know this is happening? How might previous experiences of supervision impact on the creation of an emotionally containing supervisory relationship?
4. Chair back – What are the ground rules that will help us to stay sitting up and paying attention to each other? What learning style or thinking styles do we prefer and how will we use these? What has helped us to keep focus in previous supervisions?
5. Getting in and out of the chair – At each supervision, what activity or ritual would help you settle into your chair at the start of supervision and to leave your chair at the end of supervision? Having left your supervision chair, how will we remember the main points from the supervision?
6. When will we review the continued comfort of our supervision chair?

Tool: Placement Achievements Box

The student chooses a box at the first supervision session. They could be asked to provide the box themselves or the practice educator could provide a choice of boxes. The student may choose to decorate the box in a way that is personal to them. At an agreed point in each supervision session, the practice educator asks the student to identify their 'best achievement/success' or 'special learning moment from the practice learning opportunity this week'. The practice educator or the student writes this on a chosen piece of card or paper, notes the date and adds this into the box (citizen names should not be used). The practice educator keeps the box safe throughout the practice learning opportunity and gives the completed box to the student at the final supervision.

Appendix 2

Tool: IT Bingo

Make a video call	Invite someone into a call	Set up an email signature	Turn out of office on and off
Set a reminder on your calendar	Create a Microsoft Teams meeting and invite someone to it	Create a mailing list with the people in your team in it	Set up a recurring item on your calendar
Delete an item from your calendar	Recall an email	Look up someone in the organisation's directory	Create a questionnaire in Microsoft Forms
Send a calendar invite	Raise your hand in a meeting	Send a message to everyone in a meeting	Send a message to an individual
Share your screen with someone	Create a Word document and save it on OneDrive	Work on a shared document at the same time as someone	Start a virtual whiteboard in a meeting and get someone else to draw on it
Turn your video on and off	Mute and unmute yourself	Change your background	Change your photo in your profile
Complete the mandatory training module on...	Find the emergency contact list in the shared drive and add your details	Create an Excel spreadsheet	Collaborate with someone to create a picture. Screenshot this and send to your practice educator to finish the bingo board!

Tool: Scaling tool

Working online is unhelpful for this aspect of my learning and social work practice. 	<------------------------>	This factor of my learning and social work practice is enhanced by working online. 

Share the list of words and phrases with a student. Ask them to choose where they would place each statement along the continuum. Discuss and identify which factors require addressing.

My individual factors	***My learning and support needs***
Balancing caring responsibilities	*Being supported by my practice educator*
Travel time	*Accessing training*
Looking after my physical self	*Being able to complete direct observations*
Having good routines	*Getting feedback from people who I have supported or worked with*
Balancing screen time	*Connecting with other students*
Sharing space with my family	*Having opportunities to shadow other workers*
Having quiet space to work	*Having reflective supervision*
Having an accessible workspace	*Having a range of opportunities*
Being motivated and engaged	
Recovering from stressful situations	
Knowing it is time to take a break	

→

Personal finances and access to funds for work-related expenses *Having social contact* *Finishing work and having a home life* *Being able to worship and celebrate important occasions*	*Knowing whether I am doing a good job* *Meeting the PCF standards* *Being able to try things out and make mistakes* *Having time to read and reflect* *Linking theory to practice*
My life in the team and organisation *Accessing stable internet and work-place resources* *Being able to contact people for support* *Being included* *Knowing who everyone is* *Knowing who to go to if I need help or if I've made a mistake* *Understanding the organisational values and priorities* *Keeping sensitive data safe and secure* *Seeing people 'like me' in the team or organisation, eg people of a similar age, gender, culture, religion, ethnicity or who are LGBT+* *Managing my personal vs professional online presence*	***My ability to practise effectively*** *Managing my workload* *Building relationships* *Doing direct work with people* *Helping people access the services they need* *Making accurate assessments* *Involving people who might be excluded* *Ensuring people have a voice in decisions and meetings* *Assessing housing conditions and the quality of relationships* *Helping people when they are distressed* *Treating people equally and fairly* *Using technology ethically* *Understanding people's cultural heritage* *Supporting people in the way that they choose*

Tool: Team Checklist

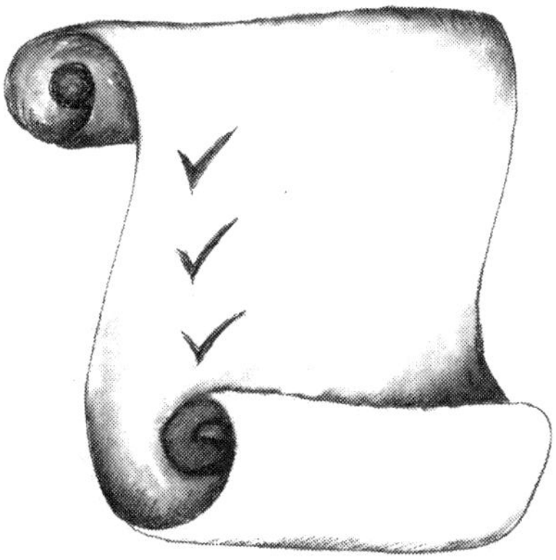

This tool identifies what practice educators and teams need to think about when preparing to welcome a student. You can use this tool to discuss things with your colleagues and set expectations.

Joining the team (team membership)	**Team Plan**
What would team members like to contribute to the plan for the student's induction period?	
When will the student meet each team member?	
What is it important for the student to see in practice? When? How will shadowing opportunities be offered and arranged? What steps need to be taken to gain consent?	
Who will the student be welcomed by on their first day?	
Which team member can act as a team buddy, eg on the days that the practice educator cannot be available?	
How will work be identified so that it fits with the student's learning needs? Who will allocate work?	
How can the team ask the student to help with specific tasks?	
Will the student take part in the duty rota? Who will support them with this?	

→

Availability	
How do the team contact each other a) in an emergency, b) with a non-urgent query, or c) if they need a debrief? What are the spoken and unspoken rules about who to contact or how?	
How will the team know where and when the student will be working? How will the student know who works on what days?	
How will the student know who is in their team when they come to the office if they have only met online before?	
Which group emails, discussion forums and calendar invites should the student be added to? Who will do this?	
Who can offer support with any technology glitches?	
How can the student be included in early days when they might not have access to the work-place systems such as email and video calling?	
Connecting for practice (co-operation)	
How will team members tell and teach the student about their roles and areas of special interest?	
What do team members hope a student will bring to the team?	
How will the student be introduced to other key people who they might need support from such as area managers or partner teams?	
Where else will students be on placement and what opportunities will there be for them to be put in touch; provide peer support or work together?	

What staff networks are available to the student and how will they be told about them? (eg LBGTQ+ network, learning and development opportunities, reading groups)	
How do the team share and talk about research and theory? Is there anything different they would like to do to support the student?	
What knowledge would the team like the student to help them update?	
Will the student have access to all of the training that the team do?	
Sensitivity	
Do the team have regular check-ins? What is the purpose and content of these? (eg service updates or informal discussion or both?)	
Who will check in with the student each day?	
How is work–life balance discussed and modelled in the team?	
Do students in your service have access to workplace counselling? Do you know what services are available to them from the university?	
How will the student's case supervision be recorded and how will they contribute to supervision discussions with allocated workers?	
What will team members do if they are concerned about the student's wellbeing?	
Acceptance	
How is difference recognised and celebrated in the team? How does the team share opinions and experiences?	
What are the different ways in which people express themselves in the team? Are any dominant in the team culture? How will the team adapt to include the student?	

→

How are successes celebrated in the team? How will team members give feedback to the student and practice educator about things they have done well?	
How can the team support the student to reflect on responses and feedback from individuals so that it shapes their learning and practice?	
Do the team know how to give feedback for the student in a way that can be incorporated into the practice educator's assessment and included in their portfolio?	
Who should the student contact if they are worried about something they have seen/heard or done?	
How are mistakes discussed and learned from in the team? Is there anything new or different in how this is managed for the student?	
At what point should the practice educator be told about concerns about the student's practice?	
Actions Required:	

Appendix 3

Tool: 'Ch-ch-ch-changes'

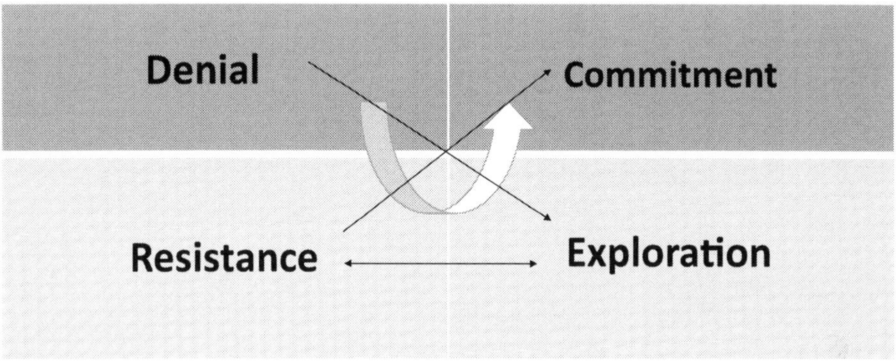

During student supervision, practice educators might discuss racism in general, or a racial incident in the local/national news, the community or on placement. The model could be applied in relation to the student's positioning on the matter, and/or to discuss feelings about the nation's perspective on the subject. The four areas of the quadrant can be explored sequentially or can relate directly to the practice educator's perception of students' responses. Remember, the student could well be in the '*exploration*' quadrant *before* the supervision session – so try to avoid making assumptions; however, the 'shock' of the incident might have returned them to *denial* or *resistance*.

Example questions (by no means exhaustive) to be asked by the practice educator (PE) include the following.

1. **Denial/Unconscious Incompetence.** Festinger suggests: we don't know what we don't know (blissful ignorance).

PE exploration – *'What is your viewpoint and understanding/interpretation of what has happened?'* (the initial response will help you to consider step 2 and so on. For example, if denial is evident, you will need to stay here and examine further).

2. **Resistance/Conscious Incompetence.** Festinger suggests: we start to become aware of what we don't know, but that knowledge is too painful; therefore, it is suppressed. This is the most difficult and unpleasant stage of the process. Consequently, we are more likely to revert to denial as it is more comfortable.

PE exploration – *'How do you feel about the incident?', 'When did you first become aware of racial difference?', 'How did/does it make you feel?', 'In terms of diversity, what did your school friendship circles look like?', 'What, if any, were the discussions around "race" and diversity like in your family growing up?', 'If you wanted to explore such matters in your family, how did it feel?', 'Who were you comfortable discussing it with (if anyone)?'*

3. **Exploration/Conscious Competence.** Festinger suggests: we become aware of what we have learnt and are keen to 'get it right'.

PE exploration – *'Why do you think you are at this stage?', 'What do you think you have learned up until now?', 'How will you know that you have not slipped back into denial or resistance?', 'What actions do think you need to take now?'*

4. **Commitment/Unconscious Competence.** Festinger suggests: we are so confident and committed to the task that we go into 'automatic pilot'.

PE exploration – *'What part do you think you have to play in anti-racism?', 'What will you do (realistically) to help to reduce the impact of racism?', 'How might this be achievable?', 'How will you* know *if this has been helpful and/or achieved?'*

Tool: 'Sheroes', 'Heroes' and 'Theyroes'

Give the student five to ten minutes to think of a superhero (or ideal childhood neighbour). You should not rush them at this point and allow maximum thinking time. Once the time is up, ask them to bullet point the character's key features. Again, allow enough time for this. Once the time is up, ask the student to share their list. Ask the student to describe the main skills, strengths, attributes, features and powers of their person of choice.

Once the student has shared the key characteristics of their person, you might ask questions such as the following.

- What inspired you to choose the person or character?
- Did you consciously select a white/black male/female/non-binary character; if so, why?
- If this was done subconsciously, why do you think this might be?
- Are you aware that when you described your person's characteristics, you included or excluded their ethnicity?
- What are your views on why there are so few black or global majorities superheroes?
- Can you see how white privilege might work in such instances?
- How do you think black people or people from the global majorities might feel about underrepresentation generally?
- On reflection, what are your thoughts and feelings now?

Tool: 'It's a Walk in the Park…'

Ask the student to close their eyes as they are about to go on a walk to the park. Ask them to imagine that they are at the front door of their home. It is a nice warm summer's day as they close the door and step outside.

1. Just as you are about to leave, the postie delivers some mail. ***Acknowledge them.***
2. You set off down the road and are immediately passed by a cyclist. ***Acknowledge them.***
3. A few minutes later, a couple, holding hands, pass you, going in the opposite direction. ***Acknowledge them.***
4. You arrive at the park and walk through the gates and pass a play area. Children are playing on the swings and in the sandpit, and parents sit close by, chatting, watching and playing with the children. ***Acknowledge them.***
5. After a while, you feel hot and thirsty so decide to get something to quench your thirst. You spot an ice-cream van nearby, where you purchase a drink and an ice-cream from the vendor. ***Acknowledge them.***
6. After a while, you decide to return home, passing the children and parents in the play area, but no one else as you make the same journey back to your front door and let yourself in.

Now, ask the student to repeat the journey aloud, but this time, ask them to *describe* the postie, the couple, the children, the parents and the ice-cream vendor.

Appendix 4

Tool: Critical Analysis of Chronologies Cards

Ask the student to reflect on a chronology they have undertaken and consider what they noticed in the recordings they drew the information from. A way of making this more engaging is to create question cards.

Here are some question examples.

How were the documents you looked at written? Did they differ in terms of tone and format for different audiences?	Did you come across jargon or acronyms? Did you understand all the terms used?
What aspects of the recordings were helpful? Why?	Did you spot documents that seemed excellent? What was it about them that you liked?
What information did you find about the person's culture, race, religion or ethnicity?	How easy or difficult was it to find the information you needed? Why?
How culturally sensitive were the documents you looked at?	How did the culture of the child, family or community inform assessments and interventions?
Imagine the documents were written about your life – how would you feel?	Did you identify any worrying patterns or trigger points?
How easy would the child or adult being written about find reading these documents? Why?	How reliable was the information you drew on? What criteria did you use to weigh information?
Why did you select the entries for the chronology? How easy or difficult was it to choose? Or to summarise?	Was any of the language used judgemental and value-laden (such as, 'mum', 'dad', 'difficult family', 'failed', 'toxic')?
Did you notice assumptions, gaps, or unsubstantiated 'facts'?	Did you see any application of theory in the documents you looked at?
How did the practice documented align with approaches and frameworks used in the practice setting?	What theories could you use to explain the documents you viewed or the chronology you created?

Tool: Lifelines and Timelines

You will need a length of wallpaper (or some sheets of paper joined together) and coloured pens. The activity can be enhanced through the use of photographs, images, stickers, or anything that could be used in a multi-media collage. You might want to ask your student to prepare by bringing some materials they want to use. Decide on a format – will this be a track, road or river? Choose a theme or purpose such as unpicking an aspect of the student's life to help them understand their experiences. Be trauma-sensitive and remember this is not therapy. Allow the student to choose what they disclose. The purpose of undertaking a lifeline activity is learning. Students need to reflect on activities and the following questions may help.

- Did anything surprise you?
- Can you identify any antecedents?
- Reflecting on the activity, can you identify when other people positively or negatively impacted on the direction of your journey?
- How did you feel undertaking the activity? How might your feelings influence the likelihood of using this tool? Or the way you might use it?
- How did the relationship with the practice educator (who holds power) influence what you disclosed or kept private?
- How does this activity fit with your culture?
- What was included? Or left out? Why might that be?
- Were you able to put things in a coherent order or are events confused?
- Can you make links to the wider context (such as attitudes and socio-political context)?
- What have you learnt that will influence your practice?
- What theories could explain any of the above?

Tool: Creating a Timeline Using Digital Tools

A PowerPoint with images, set to music and with automated slide change, can tell a powerful story. PowerPoint's 'slide-sorter' function makes it easy to add in slides and get the chronological order correct.

Choose a theme or purpose such as unpicking an aspect of the student's life to help them understand their experiences. Be trauma-sensitive and remember this is not therapy. Allow the student to choose what they disclose. The purpose of undertaking a lifeline activity is learning. Students need to reflect on activities and the following questions may help.

- Did anything surprise you?
- Can you identify any antecedents?
- Reflecting on the activity, can you identify when other people positively or negatively impacted on the direction of your journey?
- How did you feel undertaking the activity? How might your feelings influence the likelihood of using this tool? Or the way you might use it?
- How did the relationship with the practice educator (who holds power) influence what you disclosed or kept private?
- How does this activity fit with your culture?
- What was included? Or left out? Why might that be?
- Were you able to put things in a coherent order or are events confused?
- Can you make links to the wider context (such as attitudes and socio-political context)?
- What have you learnt that will influence your practice?
- What theories could explain any of the above?

Tool: Creating a Timeline or Trajectory Using Home Resources

Share with the student some information about timelines and trajectories before asking for this to be created at home. The document, or photograph of their artefact, can then be shared with you or, if working with a group of students, on a closed group using Padlet®, which is a free online pinboard. Students can use any means they wish, including going outside, and can choose what aspect, ie looking forward or back, to explore. Following this activity, students could be asked to complete a written reflective evaluation to add another dimension to their learning or use the questions from the second and third tools.

Appendix 5

Tool: Purpose, Position and Power

Part 1: Purpose

Reflective activity for a practice educator part 1: Purpose
❖ What motivated you to become a practice educator? ❖ Make a list of at least five reasons why you decided to become a practice educator. ❖ Have any of these reasons changed over time? Why? Why not? ❖ What keeps you motivated as a practice educator?

Reflective activity for a practice educator to use with a student part 1: Purpose
Practice educators can begin this activity by asking students to list the reasons they decided to undertake their social work training. This is a question I ask early in the practice learning opportunity, and sometimes at the pre-placement meeting, as it often provides a valuable insight into the desires and motivations of students. Knowing this helps me to tailor the learning opportunities that can be made available to the student. This question also begins to explore concepts of power, which can be revisited during supervision sessions using the reflective activities within this tool. It is interesting to revisit the question at the end of the practice learning opportunity to see if the student has changed their thoughts in any way.

Part 2: Position

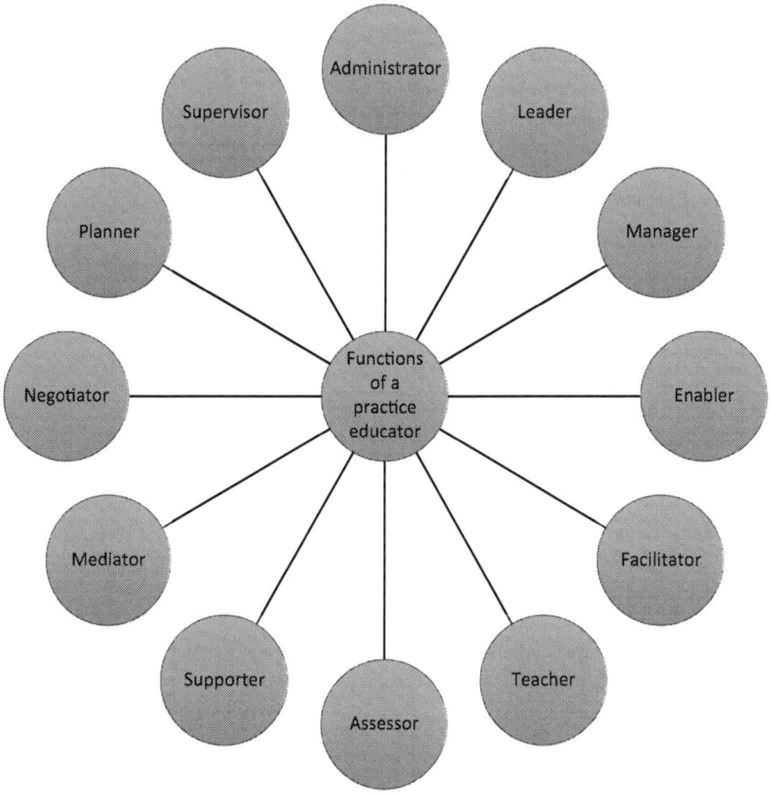

Reflective activity to be undertaken by a practice educator part 2: Position
Look at the different functions involved in the practice education role. You may wish to add more to the list. Identify the aspects you feel more comfortable with. For example, you may feel more comfortable seeing yourself as a Facilitator of learning rather than a Gatekeeper, or vice versa. You could number these from 1 to 12, with 12 being what you feel most comfortable with. After you have considered which of the functions you are more comfortable undertaking, develop your professional curiosity by answering the following questions. ❖ I am more comfortable with these aspects of the practice education role because... ❖ I am less comfortable with these aspects of the practice education role because...

- Have my thoughts about the different aspects of the role changed over time? Why? Why not?
- Does my level of comfort change depending on the individual characteristics of the student? Why? Why not?
- What if aspects of their identity such as ethnicity, gender, age, class or sexuality differ from mine? Does this make a difference to how I feel? Why? Why not?
- To become more comfortable with some of the functions of a practice educator I need to ...
- Is there anything else I need to do move out of my comfort zone to ensure that I am using the legitimate authority which is inherent within the role?

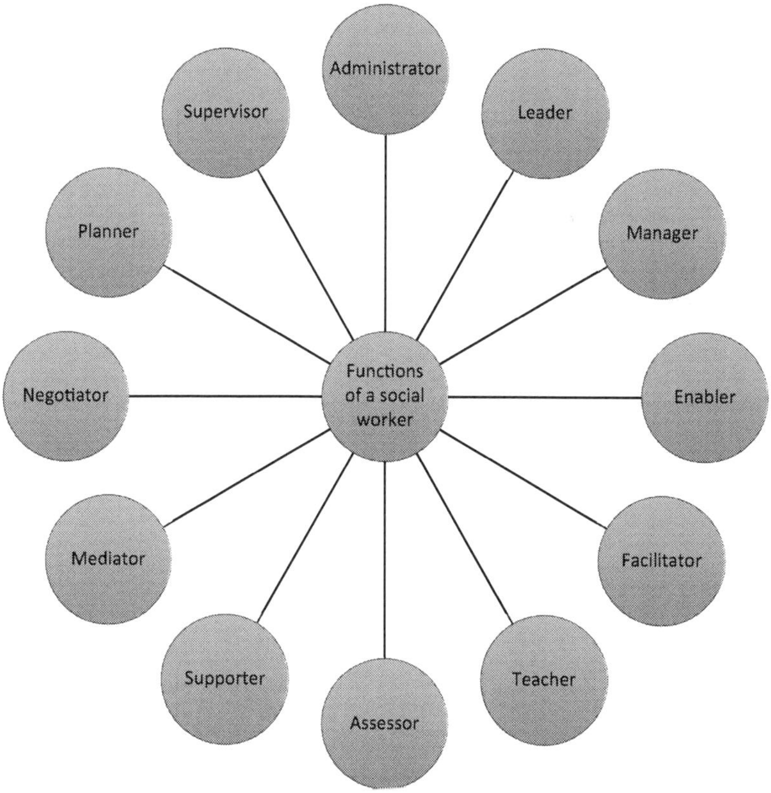

Reflective activity for a practice educator to use with a student part 2: Position
The Position activity can be adapted by practice educators to explore how comfortable students are with the power linked to the legitimate authority they hold as a social work student. The various roles of a social worker could be discussed (see above) and the student asked if there are any others they feel should be added to the list. The student is then asked to number the functions from 1 to 12, with 12 being one that the student feels most comfortable with. Ideas of positional power can then be introduced using the following questions to promote a reflective discussion. ❖ I am more comfortable with these aspects of the social work role because... ❖ I am less comfortable with these aspects of the social work role because... ❖ To become more comfortable with some of the functions of a social worker, during this placement I need to... ❖ Does my level of comfort change depending on the characteristics of the individuals I am working with? Why? Why not? ❖ What if aspects of their identity such as ethnicity, gender, age, class or sexuality differ from mine? Does this make a difference to how I feel? Why? Why not? ❖ Is there anything I need to do in relation to this to be effective in my role as a social work student?

Part 3: Power

Reflective activity for a practice educator part 3: Power

As practice educators it is important to reflect on our own internal world as this can help us to tune in to the range of feelings and worries that a student may be experiencing (Finch, 2017). Working with students can produce a range of emotions and feelings for practice educators, particularly when working with students who may be struggling.

- Look at the images and identify one that reflects your feelings when a student is on track to pass the practice placement.
- Now pick an image that reflects your feelings when you are working with a student and there is a possibility that they could fail the placement.
- Was it easy to find an image to represent a successful student? Why?
- Was it more difficult to identify an image that reflected a student who may be struggling? Why? Why not?
- Are you able to make any connections with how you feel about the different functions of the practice educator role?
- How does this relate to concepts of power discussed within this chapter?

Tool: Power and Rights-based Triangle

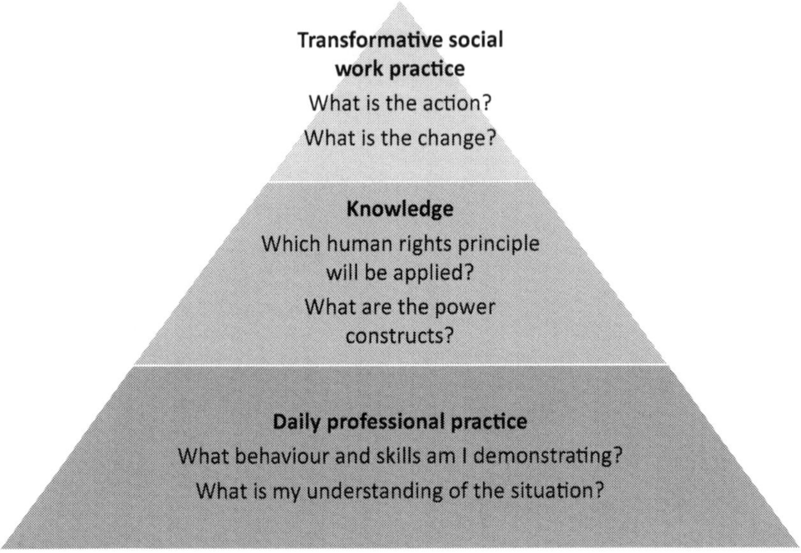
Transformative social work practice
What is the action?
What is the change?
Knowledge
Which human rights principle will be applied?
What are the power constructs?
Daily professional practice
What behaviour and skills am I demonstrating?
What is my understanding of the situation?

Daily professional practice

Questions to explore daily professional practice	
What is my understanding? Deconstruction of the situation	1. What is happening? 2. How might the situation be understood differently from the practice educator's/ individual's perspective?
Behaviours and skills demonstrated Development of insight	1. How am I exercising power? 2. How am I participating within the situation? eg am I participating with the individual or am I expecting them to participate with me? Is the participation meaningful, inclusive with shared accountability or one-sided, tokenistic and consultative? 3. What behaviours and skills am I demonstrating? 4. What are the implicit assumptions or knowledge within the situation? Is this influencing the situation? 5. What is working well?

Knowledge

Questions to break down the power constructs	
Power to Aspects which help to create change and achieve goals	1. How am I positioned to access power? So, what are my characteristics and/or privileges – *ethnicity, class, gender, socioeconomic status, ability, sexual orientation, education and background.* 2. Where do I draw power from in terms of my social work role? eg position, professional status, organisational context, legal authority, academic qualification, knowledge and/or the state. 3. What else helps me feel empowered within this relationship?
Power over How power is exercised and possessed	1. Does the relationship feel hierarchical and imbalanced? If so, please explain. 2. Does the relationship include resistance and conflict? If so, please explain. 3. Does the relationship feel negotiated and reciprocal? If so, please explain. 4. Can you identify any structural aspects which impact the situation? eg workplace culture, bureaucratic policies and processes, management ethos. 5. Is there a difference between my interests and those of the individual/practice educator? 6. Is there a legitimate use of power through my use of authority?
Power with Greater power through collaboration	1. What are the values that I present within this relationship? eg partnership with a shared/balanced level of power with respect, mutual support and collaboration to build bridges and across difference. 2. How do I learn within this relationship?

→

Power from within Recognition of self-worth and drawing on inner strength	1. What do I have that equips me when faced with challenges? 2. What helps me to overcome obstacles?

Areas of exploration to break down the human rights principles (United Nations Human Rights, Office of the High Commissioner, nd and adapted from Androff, 2018)	
Dignity *Article 1 Free and equal* *Article 3 Right to life* *Article 4 Freedom from slavery* *Article 5 Freedom from torture* *Article 12 Right to privacy*	1. Recognition of ways that the individual has been respected, or dehumanised, stigmatised or blamed. 2. What 'lens' is being applied and how does it explain/support the situation? eg passive gifting of support or active, capable rights-holder? 3. Draw upon the Code of Ethics (BASW, 2021).
Non-discrimination *Article 2 Freedom from discrimination* *Article 6 Right to recognition before the law* *Article 7 Right to equality before the law* *Article 8 Access to justice* *Article 9 Freedom from arbitrary detention* *Article 11 Presumption of innocence* *Article 14 Right to asylum* *Article 18 Freedom of religion or belief*	1. Consideration of the protected characteristics, eg gender, age, sexual orientation, etc (see Equality and Human Rights Commission, 2021 for more information). 2. Considerations of inclusion and exclusion, including historic notions of marginalisation. 3. Ways in which practice is understood to be culturally appropriate. 4. Exploration of how identity and diversity shape human experience. 5. Recognition of privilege(s).

Participation *Article 13 Freedom of movement* *Article 16 Right to marriage and to found a family* *Article 17 Right to own a property* *Article 20 Freedom of assembly* *Article 21 Right to partake in public affairs* *Article 22 Right to social security* *Article 23 Right to work* *Article 24 Right to leisure and rest* *Article 25 Right to adequate standard of living* *Article 26 Right to education* *Article 27 Right to take part in cultural, artistic and scientific life* *Article 28 Right to a free and fair world*	1. Explore ways in which the individual has influence and input into decisions which affect them. 2. Is participation tokenistic or genuine and meaningful? How have you reached this conclusion? 3. You may find Arnstein's Ladder of Citizen Participation helpful to refer to within this section (Arnstein, 1969, cited in Organizing Engagement, 2021) 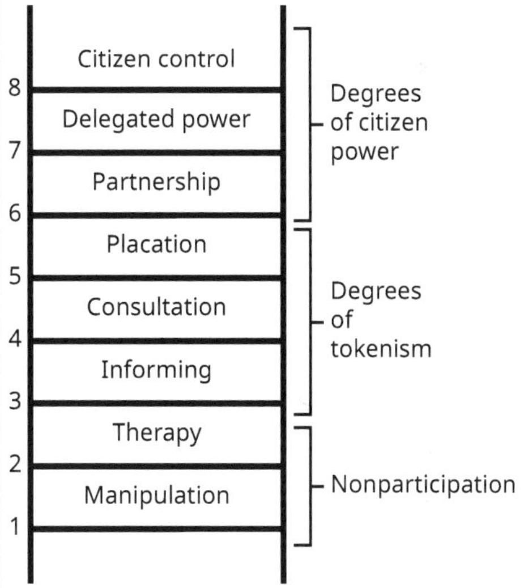

→

Transparency *Article 10 Right to a fair trial* *Article 19 Freedom of expression*	1. Consideration of processes, policies and budget transparency and the influence upon the working relationship. 2. Discussion of rationales, evidence-based decisions, assessments and judgements. 3. Implementing reflexivity and critically reflective skills.
Accountability *Article 15 Right to nationality* *Article 29 Duty to your community* *Article 30 Rights are inalienable*	1. Utilising legislation and research to enhance professional credibility. 2. Consideration of the way in which you advocate, empower and inform individuals. 3. Exploring ways in which to contribute towards a rights-based culture.

Transformative social work practice

Questions to explore the next steps	
What is the change? What direction do you want to take?	1. What is the desired goal?
What is the action? How this will be achieved	1. How will this be achieved? 2. What do I need to move towards the intended goal? Who will help me?

Appendix 6

Tool: 'The Stripper' story

Ask the student to read this story.

I begin my first story... you know that my son Fabian is great at playing the piano. In fact, no one taught him how to play; he just sat down one day and played. He was watching his sister painstakingly trying to pick out the notes of a tune on the piano and then he waited for her to get up from the piano stool. He then went and sat down at the stool and played the piece with both hands. You see, it is hard being a child with additional needs when your older sister is good at so many things. So, when you see her finding something hard and you know you can do it, it becomes sweet justice to just go over, take a seat and play the piece with ease. After that he set his sights on being an organist.

When my son was younger, the church that we attended had a service for older members of the community three times a year. It was Fabian's joy and privilege to be able to be the organist for this service. In the week before the Easter service, my son kept teasing me, saying he was going to play the wrong music at the service. I thought he was joking, but he kept on with it. The Easter service is quite sombre and, as the vicar announced the second hymn, I saw Fabian chuckle to himself. Then, instead of playing the hymn 'Amazing Grace', I could hear him strike up the opening chords of a completely different tune. To my absolute horror, I recognised the opening bars of 'The Stripper'! I took hold of his hands and said, 'No, play the hymn'. I let go of his hands and again he started to play 'The Stripper'. I took his hands again and said, 'Last chance'. I could see the congregation of older people who had struggled to their feet to sing patiently waiting. Once again, he played the opening bars of 'The Stripper'. I just wanted the ground to open up and swallow me in that moment; I was so embarrassed. There was a complete hush in the church and the vicar was looking at us wondering what was happening. I turned to Fabian and told him that he was going home with his dad and that I would play for the rest of the service.

Later in the day (after I had calmed down a bit), I asked Fabian why he had done that. For the first time in his life, he told me the reason. Six days earlier, I had refused to park my car in the place that he had requested. So, he had 'kept his powder dry' for six days and then unleashed his revenge in public. However, instead of being angry about this, I saw an opportunity. 'I understand that you were angry with me over the parking', I said, 'but you took it out on everyone in the church. The people who came for a service had to wait while you played the wrong thing; the vicar may well have felt embarrassed too. Was that fair?' His face fell as he realised what he had done, and again that day, I realised that there was another first. I also realised that his choice of music had been because of its complete inappropriateness for the occasion. I realised that he knew what appropriate and inappropriate meant. So, we had a conversation about this too. Suddenly, I realised that what had been an excruciatingly embarrassing afternoon was not so bad after all. In fact, nobody died, and most people were laughing about it. It became a bit of a joke to see who knew which tune it was that Fabian was playing.

Activity 1: Reframing activity

Discuss how reframing a situation can have a powerful impact. Students could then relate their thoughts to an experience of their own.

What happened (fact/ observation)	My interpretation (these are not facts)	My feelings are:	Another alternative interpretation (these are not facts)	My feelings would be:

Activity 2: Reflective activity

As a practice educator, ask the student to spend 15 minutes of their reflective time each day for four consecutive days to write about the following.

Imagine a time, five years from now, when everything that you hope for now has been accomplished. Try to be as specific as you can and write about what your life will be like. Try not to censor yourself as you write. This is about you being your best self. Consider your career, your academic work, relationships, finances, family, friends and anything else that is important to you. Be as specific as you can – the more detail the better.

You could also use these coaching questions (Biswas-Diener, 2010) to help the student to gain more from the exercise.

- How important is it to you to achieve the 'ideal self'?
- When are you planning to make the changes associated with achieving the 'ideal self'?
- What resources and opportunities do you have that will help you work towards your 'ideal self'?
- What hurdles do you anticipate? How can these be part of the growth process?
- What factors inform your vision of your 'ideal self'?
- How internal (as opposed to external) are the values that inform your 'ideal self'?
- What person, living or dead, is similar to your 'ideal self'?
- Name a single small behaviour you can change as a first step towards your 'ideal self'.
- How can you chart your progress towards your 'ideal self'?

Tool: The Boxing Day story

Ask the student to read this story.

There was one year, just after we had completed a lot of building work on the house. It was Boxing Day and the family were watching an afternoon film on the TV. Fabian wasn't interested in the film, so he was playing quietly in his bedroom – or so we thought.

Suddenly, the lights went off and the TV went off, and we could hear shrieking coming from upstairs. Then there was an almighty crash as a ceiling fell in. I rushed upstairs to find my son. He was standing in the bathroom ankle deep in water with a large lemonade bottle in his hand. He had been filling the bottle from the bath tap and then tipping it onto the floor. Immediately, I realised what the crash was and also just how much water he had poured onto the floor, which had now rendered the house uninhabitable – on Boxing Day.

Reflective activity

Suggest a piece of the student's reflective time is used to write about something that happened during their practice learning opportunity that did not go the way they had planned, or which had taken them by surprise. They need to be prepared to share this within their next supervision. During the session, ask the student to take a pen and highlight the judgements they made about themselves. These may be things where the student has used words such as 'like', 'should have', 'must do', 'need to', 'right/wrong', 'appropriate/inappropriate' and 'good/bad'.

Then ask the student to consider how judging the event serves them – what are they wanting to achieve? Once we uncover the role of the judgement, we can find another way to achieve the things that we want by framing these in a more positive way. The last part of the exercise can be to ask the student to consider what difference it makes for them to be kinder to themselves and to consider reflecting without judgement or blame.

You may wish to ask the student to start with something small and then build up to consider bigger things. Remind the student not to judge the judgement but just take the time to understand themselves through this exercise.

Tool: The Musician story

Ask the student to read this story.

Way back now, you will remember that we home schooled Fabian using a therapy programme. Part of that programme involved deciding that whatever he decided to do had meaning, purpose and value even if I didn't know what that was. It also showed him that I valued his choices and that there was nowhere that he could choose to go where I would not want to go with him. To do this though, I needed to be present in the moment and to focus completely on his activity so I could closely follow what he was doing. In the early days of the programme, he would walk in circles around the edge of the room writing in the air with his finger. This activity went on for weeks if not months. As I wanted to connect with him and to encourage him to play with me, I did the same thing as him. This was more than just copying; it was a sincere attempt to join in with his game. It was a way to find out what his motivations were because he couldn't tell me at the time.

One night after spending most of the day doing this activity, I decided to take a long hot bath. While lying there in the water my thoughts drifted to a band rehearsal that I had recently been to, where we listened to a new song that we were going to learn. As I was recalling the song, I realised that I was writing in the air in the same way as I had been doing all day with Fabian. Then I wondered, 'but what if he is walking around thinking about music all day too?'

So, the next day, I was walking with Fabian around in circles writing in the air. This time though I started to put notes to his movements and to make a tune. Before too long, I realised the tune – it was Tchaikowsky's 1812 overture. My son went on to become an accomplished pianist and I think that all those months spent walking around the room allowed him to build the gross motor patterns that he then called on to play the piano from scratch. Playing the piano has given him a social role in groups as 'Mr Music Man'. It has been something that he is good at and has given his self-esteem a massive boost. All of this would not have happened if we had not been present and stayed with him when he was doing something that I didn't understand. If I had been concerned in those days about whether he might one day live independently or focused on all of the things he couldn't do, I would have missed the thing he actually could do. This is the lesson of mindfulness.

Activity

The Musician Story can promote a discussion about the need to be present within social work, as well as part of self-care.

This exercise can be used as part of supervision or the student could be asked to do this as a personal activity during their reflective time.

Gather some inexpensive craft materials or ask the student to find some bits and pieces that they can use to make something of beauty. Some suggestions are to download a mandala to colour or use some paints to create a picture. Ask the student to completely immerse themselves in the process of creation, knowing that whatever they make is for this moment only and more for the experience of creation rather than for the outcome. Suggest to the student that if they find their mind drifting onto other things, to gently, without judgement, come back to the activity. Mindfulness is not something we can do straight away; that is why it is known as a practice.

Then, when the piece has been created, ask the student to destroy it and reflect on the experience, either individually or in supervision with you, by considering the following questions.

- How did it feel to create something impermanent?
- How did you feel destroying it?
- What difference do you think this activity might make to how you view events during your working day?
- Who are you letting decide your value?
- Who decides how valuable what you do is?
- What connections can you make to your social work practice?

Appendix 7

Tool: Assumptions Checklist

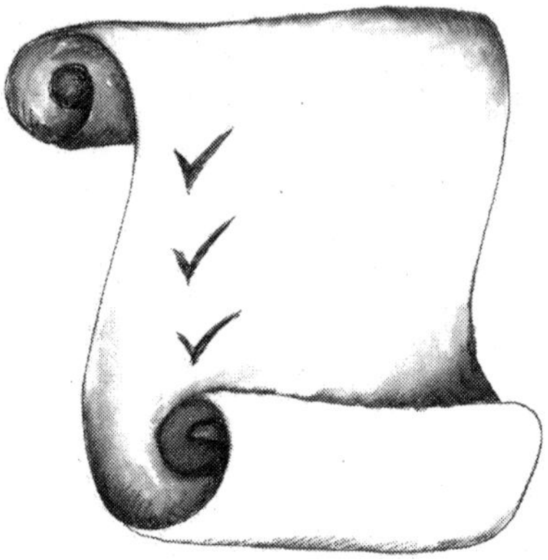

Practice educators need to accept and respect students' circumstances and understand how these impact on the learning and assessment process. This exercise works well if it takes place within a supportive and open professional relationship. What it has the potential to do is to provide an opportunity for discussion, mutual learning and self-awareness.

Question (to ask of each other)	**Answer**
1. What kinds of music do I like?	
2. What is my favourite colour?	
3. Which political party do I affiliate to?	
4. What kinds of films do I enjoy watching?	
5. What is my social class?	
6. What kinds of books do I enjoy reading?	
7. Do I prefer the country or the city?	
8. How old am I?	
9. Do I observe a religious doctrine?	
10. Am I trans or cis gender?	
11. What hobbies do I have?	
12. Was I brought up in care?	
13. Do I prefer dogs, cats or neither?	
14. Do I enjoy sporting activities?	

15. Do I watch television?	
16. Do I celebrate Christmas?	
17. How many countries have I visited?	
18. Was I born in the UK?	
19. Which newspapers do I read?	
20. What is my favourite type of food?	

Tool: Professional Curiosity Self-assessment Checklist

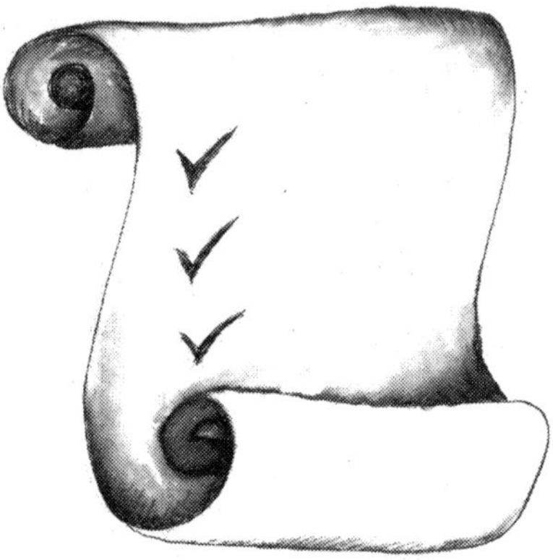

This tool can be used individually or jointly and reflexively discussed. It is important to complete the column 'What helps me to achieve this?', which can form the basis of discussion taking place within the professional supervision relationship and set out the support needed to develop professional capability.

Beliefs about my professional curiosity	**Yes? No? Maybe?**	**Indicator**	**What helps me to achieve this?**	**What gets in the way?**
I am curious and inquisitive about what I see, hear, think and feel and about what appears to be missing.		• Aware when assumptions are being made so as not to act on them. • Actively listen and make connections. • Take a holistic approach. • Aware of inconsistencies.		

Beliefs about my professional curiosity	Yes? No? Maybe?	Indicator	What helps me to achieve this?	What gets in the way?
I try to understand the context, process and content of information I receive.		• Explore ideas and reflect on information. • Do not take things at face value. • See social situ-ations as complex.		
I look for new information that may disconfirm my initial views about situations particularly where there is identified risk.		• Aware that I make mistakes. • Inform others, and apologise when mistakes are made. • Enjoy learning. • Open to feedback. • Avoid the use of blame.		
I am prepared to change my mind about a person or situation.		• Accept that things are uncertain. • Open to new information. • Manage anxieties well.		
I acknow-ledge my power and privilege.		• Recognise, discuss and challenge 'isms', eg racism, sexism, ageism, disablism, childism, classism, heterosexism.		

→

Beliefs about my professional curiosity	**Yes? No? Maybe?**	**Indicator**	**What helps me to achieve this?**	**What gets in the way?**
I am healthily sceptical about the things I read and hear.		• Look for inconsistencies. • Look for alternative perspectives.		
I respectfully challenge people's ideas if I disagree with or am unsure about them.		• Aware of conflict avoidance and unconscious bias.		
I think critically about cultural contexts and try to make what is implicit explicit.		• Aware of cultural relativism. • Understand culture as tacit. • Aware of professional dangerousness.		
I talk to influential others about concerns and questions about practice.		• Reflect with others who help me to see different perspectives and who provoke deeper thinking.		

Tool: Professional Curiosity and Professional Context Checklist

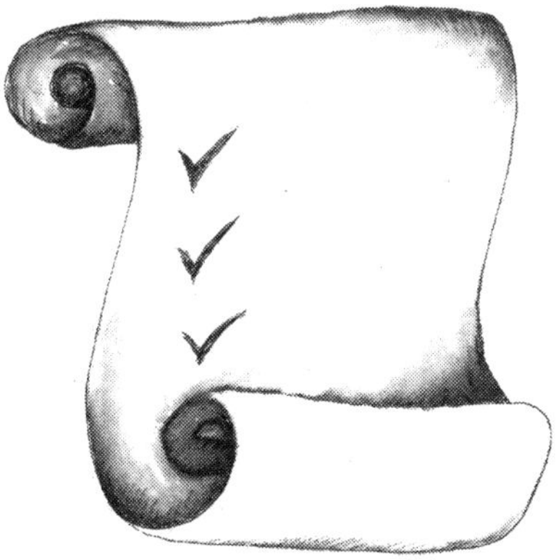

This tool helps social work students and practice educators to identify and think about the role of organisational contexts in supporting or hampering the practice and development of professional curiosity. The questions should be used to explore how things are and what might be different. This might involve checking with a student their value of the information as well as the degree of confidence, certainty and/or uncertainty of their knowledge or understanding and what might be missing. It also involves sharing the rationale that curiosity is enhanced or diminished under certain conditions.

Beliefs about my professional context	**Yes? No? Maybe?**	**Indicator**	**What can I do to improve the situation?**	**What gets in the way?**
I am supported by my practice educator/ supervisor/ manager and team.		• Discussions about practice concerns and dilemmas take place regularly. • I learn from discussions.		

→

Beliefs about my professional context	**Yes? No? Maybe?**	**Indicator**	**What can I do to improve the situation?**	**What gets in the way?**
The team or organisation where I am placed/work is stable and consistent.		• The team or organisation where I am placed/work is not going through a restructure or major change process.		
I am able to openly discuss fears and concerns about my work with my colleagues and practice educator/ supervisors/ managers.		• Communication is open in the team or organisation where I work. • People are not worried about being blamed when things go wrong. • The team is supportive.		
I get time to think and reflect.		• Workload is manageable.		
I get regular good-quality supervision.		• Supervision balances personal and professional development, and management of tasks and targets.		

Beliefs about my profes-sional context	Yes? No? Maybe?	Indicator	What can I do to improve the situation?	What gets in the way?
I have good professional relationships with colleagues from other teams and disciplines.		• Sharing information with other professionals is open and works well.		
I keep good-quality contemporaneous records of contacts made with individuals and professionals.		• Records are written directly after contact with, or about, a child or adult. • Records are written in a way that acknowledges the person who they are about may read them.		

Appendix 8

Tool: Endings Sensory Stick Person

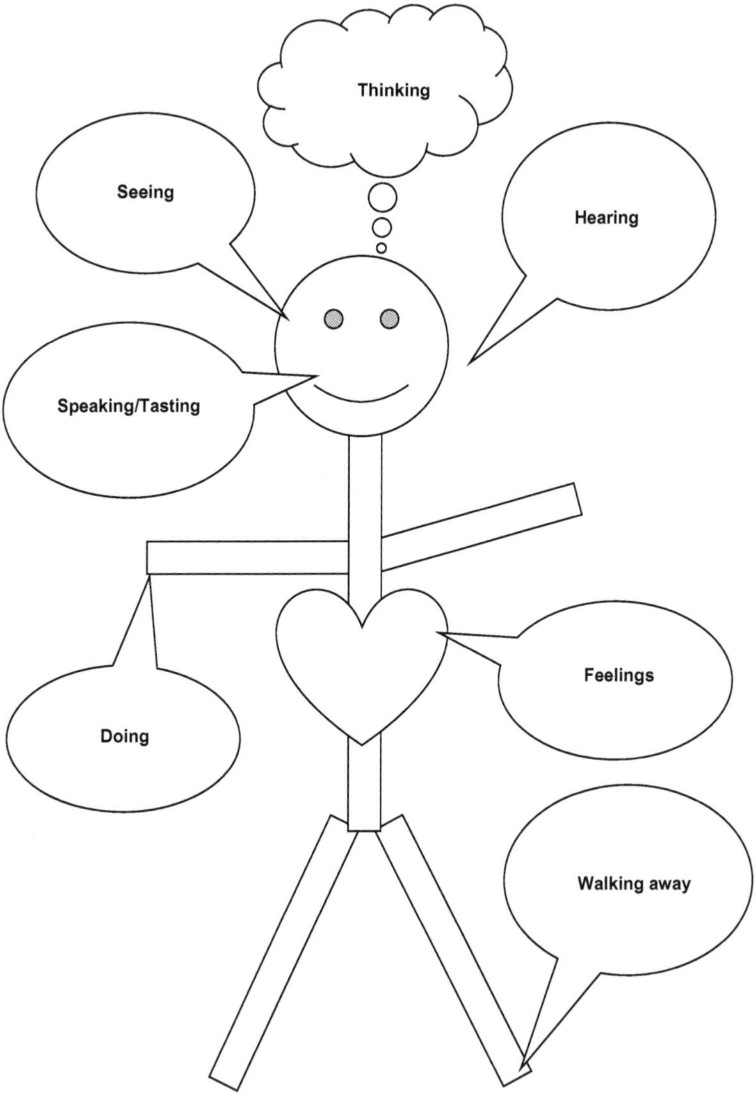

When working virtually, the **Endings Sensory Stick Person** template can be shared online and completed electronically. When working in person, the student can draw themselves as a stick person on a large sheet of paper, decorate as they wish, and the discussion is recorded in speech bubbles around the drawing.

For each speech bubble the practice educator guides the conversation.

Thinking (head) – This is a sensitive area of discussion and needs to be managed with care. It can be offered as an opportunity for the student to think about how their own experiences of endings may influence their reactions to professional endings. Questions that could be useful are:

- what memories or thoughts do you have about previous endings?
- how might those memories or thoughts influence this ending?

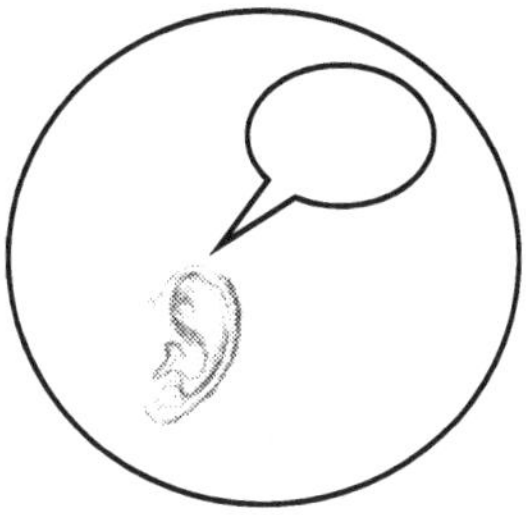

Hearing (ears) – This provides an opportunity for the student to think about what they would like to hear about at the end of their practice learning opportunity and from whom. Useful questions could be:

- what would you like to hear about when we end our work?
- who would you like to hear from?
- why might it be important to hear from that person?

Seeing (eyes) – This is an opportunity to visualise the end or the final day of the practice learning opportunity. The practice educator might ask questions such as:

- what would you like your ending to look like?
- who would you like to see on your final day? And why?

Speaking and tasting (mouth) – This is an opportunity to think about who the student may wish to speak with at the end of the practice learning opportunity and how this will be achieved. Useful questions might be:

- what might you like to say when we end our work?
- who will you need to speak to?
- how will we ensure there is an opportunity to do that?

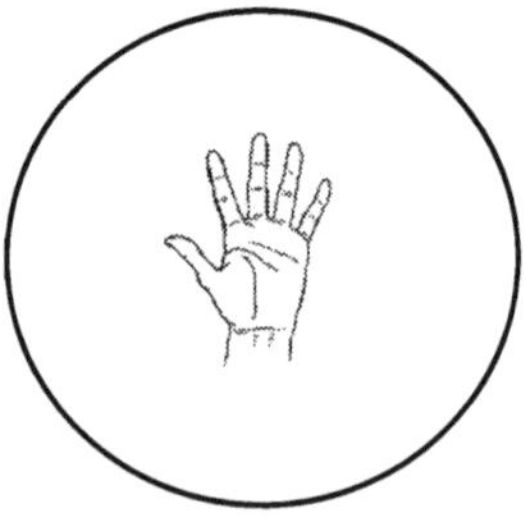

Doing (hands) – This section provides an opportunity to discuss what the student might like to do with the team, practice educator or individuals to mark the end of their practice learning opportunity. It might also include how the student will start preparing individuals for the end of their working relationship. Useful questions may be:

- what do we need to do before our ending?
- what would you like to do on your final day/week to mark your ending?
- how will you involve each individual in planning for the end of your work together?

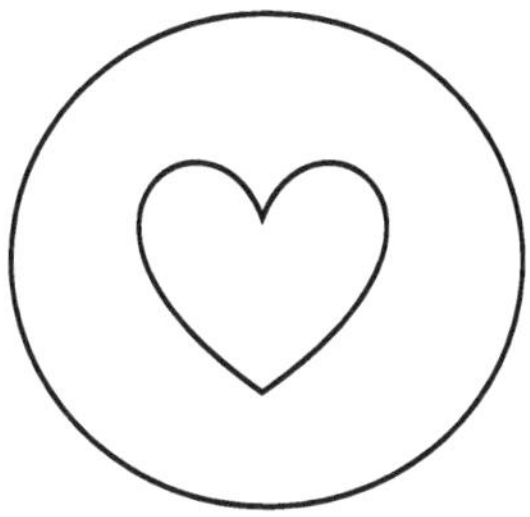

Feelings (heart) – In this section the practice educator and student discuss feelings associated with the end of the practice learning opportunity. Discussions from the 'thinking' section of the activity may be interwoven with this part of the activity. Questions that could be helpful are:

- what do you feel right now about ending the practice learning opportunity?
- what might you feel as you near the final day?
- why might you feel that way?
- how might you manage those feelings?
- who might support you with that?
- how might you express those feelings?

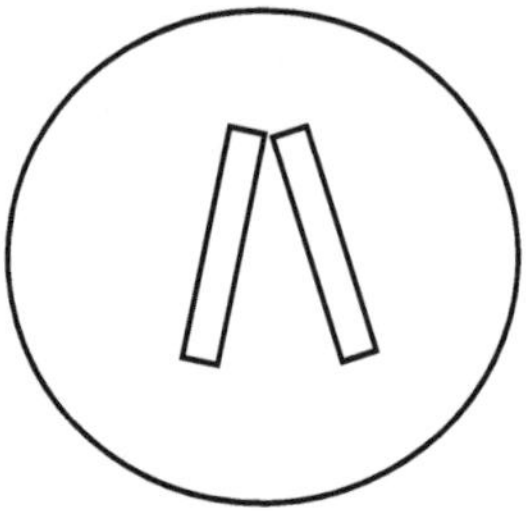

Walking away (feet) – This section of the discussion focuses on how to ensure the student will walk away from the practice learning opportunity with what they need for the future. This area of the discussion is also helpful for planning any outstanding learning needs for the second part of the practice learning opportunity. Revisiting the **Endings Sensory Stick Person** at future supervisions will help to review these. Helpful questions could include:

- what new learning do you want to achieve before you walk away?
- how might you do that?
- how will you know this has happened?
- imagining moving on from this practice learning opportunity, what will you carry with you in your toolkit?
- what might make it hard to walk away?
- what would make it easier?

Tool: End of Placement Reflection Letter

A letter to yourself from yourself for both the practice educator and the student to complete.

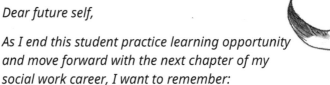

Dear future self,

As I end this student practice learning opportunity and move forward with the next chapter of my social work career, I want to remember:

Experiences

What were my most positive experiences?

Why were they positive?

How have they impacted on me?

Feelings

What feelings have I experienced during this practice learning opportunity?

Why did I feel this way?

How did I manage these feelings?

Values and beliefs

What values and beliefs have been important to me?

Why were they important?

How will I hold onto these?

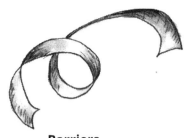

Barriers

What barriers did I face? What were these related to?

Why did these barriers arise?

How did I manage these barriers or overcome them?

Learning

What is my biggest learning?

Why is this my biggest learning?

How has it influenced my practice?

Skills and tools

What new skills and tools have I developed?

Why are they useful?

How will I take these forward?

My best advice from this practice learning opportunity experience:

Tool: Placement Memory Jar

Materials needed:

- a range of small clean spice/mini jam jars;
- table salt;
- coloured chalk sticks;
- sticky tape;
- A4 paper;
- table cover.

Invite the student to choose a jar. The student chooses approximately the correct amount of table salt to fill the jar. They spend some time thinking about five memories from the practice learning opportunity. These could be five stages they have identified over the practice learning opportunity, five feelings, five significant pieces of work, five pieces of learning, a mixture of all of these or something else. The student then divides the salt into five separate amounts and each is placed on a separate piece of A4 paper. These will form the five layers to represent the identified memories. Some memories might be more significant than others and this can be reflected in the size of the layer (so more salt for the more significant memories).

Each layer of salt should be a different colour; the student should reflect on which colour is most appropriate. For example, the student may associate a certain colour with a feeling, piece of work or learning. Taking one of the five amounts of salt and holding the chosen coloured chalk stick in a vertical position, the chalk stick is rubbed over the salt to colour it. Glitter could also be added if desired. The longer the chalk is rubbed over the salt, the deeper the shade of the colour. When the layer of salt is coloured, the student lifts the A4 paper with the coloured salt on it and, holding it rather like a funnel, pours it into the jar. Knock the jar gently on the table to help the salt to settle. This is repeated for the five layers.

The conversation with the student while they are making the **Placement Memory Jar** or after the jar is completed is vital to gain the most reflection and learning from the activity. For example, some of the following questions could be useful.

- What did you feel?
- What impact did that have?
- What might the impact of that be moving forward?
- Why do you think you felt like that?
- Why was that a positive moment for you?
- Why do you think your feelings changed?
- Why do you think you responded in that way?
- How might you manage those feelings?
- How might those feelings impact on you using the activity with people with lived experience?
- How do you feel about that now?
- How did you know that?

When the jar is completed, the lid of the jar is replaced and strengthened by adding clear sticky tape around it. The student then makes a decorative note to accompany the jar, listing the meaning of each layer.

Tool: Appreciative Present Posters

An **Appreciative Present Poster** is a gift for the student to mark the end of the practice learning opportunity and is created by the practice educator and their team for the student.

A large sheet of paper is required, and a present box with ribbon and gift tag is drawn onto the paper for the student. Each person who is saying 'goodbye' to the student writes a personal message on the present. This should be specific to the student and describe something positive they have appreciated or noticed about them. For example, 'I liked the way you always said hello in the mornings' or 'I noticed when you worked with H, you always gave him time to talk'. When complete, the **Appreciative Present Poster** can be given to the student in a number of ways, depending on what is appropriate. However, making the poster feel special, like a present, is important. Like an end of work letter, it could be rolled up, tied with a ribbon and presented at a leaving event or sent in the mail as a surprise. For virtual working, appreciative comments could be collected from team members online and inserted into a Word document version of the present or a PowerPoint presentation with meaningful music added.

Index